A Fairy Godmom's Book of Reminders

Trusting What You Know About Being a Mom

by Julie Wheaton & Patrece Powers

Published by
Two Tigers Ink

Post Office Box 12754
La Jolla, California 92039-2754

Printed on recycled paper (30% post consumer).
ISBN 0-9754494-0-0

Contents

I was a woman first.

Then a lover,

Then a mother,

And now I understand what it means
to be a woman first.

— *Julie Wheaton*

All Mom

FOUR YEARS OF MOTHERHOOD HAD PASSED BEFORE
THE THOUGHT OF ENJOYMENT CROSSED MY MIND.

For the first three, I was just getting through it. I was
adjusting to so many changes at once: the physical demands,
the sleep deprivation, the housework, the emotional roller
coaster, the fear, the loneliness, and the most difficult part
for me—the sense that there was no way out—at least for
another 18 years or so.

The miniscule mosaic of self-identity that I had pieced
together at age 24 began to erode after I gave birth to my

first child. Before I became a mom, the image I had of life with a baby was something like this:

First, I'd be stepping into a new phase of my life. That alone was exciting. I was going to be somebody's MOM. The media said that I would glow with natural beauty, wear great-looking maternity clothes, and decorate an adorable nursery.

Second, I would have a beautiful, healthy baby (maybe twins). Would it be a boy or a girl? Who would it look like? Of course, there was that small detail about giving birth. No big deal, though. I'd heard that, with the advances in pain management, some women played cards during labor. I could do that.

And finally, I knew I'd be a great mom because I was the oldest of three siblings and I currently owned two dogs. In fact, I'd owned five dogs at once and, aside from a large bill at the feed store, I managed just fine. Having a dog is a lot like having a baby, right?

In my image of life with a baby, my husband would be moved by my natural glow and womanly state. He would work to support our growing family, while I would spend my days sewing curtains, doing scrapbooks, and cooking meals. I would dance through my household responsibilities with a baby in tow. No commute to work. No bosses. No pantyhose. Just me and my baby doing the grocery shopping, going to the park, walking the dogs, and blissfully enjoying each other.

——————— *Screech!!* ———————

Now here's what really happened:

My "natural glow" was pale green. I was so nauseous for the first three months that I couldn't cook. Most of our meals were around a table at Subway. I had to go potty constantly, which meant that I confined my fitness walks to new housing developments because they had porta-potties.

My "great-looking maternity clothes" consisted of borrowed classics, my husband's shirts, and the occasional sale item from Target's maternity department. I was determined not to own maternity underwear. One evening as I changed into my nightgown, my husband looked over at me. I readied myself for a compliment on my womanly state. Instead he blurted out, "What's that on your belly?" I looked down, and there, at waistband-level embossed in my flesh were the words "Victoria's Secret." The next day, I went to the maternity store and bought a three-pack of parachutes.

The "adorable nursery" consisted of a white, wooden crib and a matching rocking chair. The bathroom counter doubled as the changing table. Over the years, the nursery moved from a corner in our one-bedroom condo to a small bedroom with rust-colored shag carpeting from 1977.

During my first pregnancy, I attended the hospital's presentation on pain management. I was horrified at what I saw in films on the birth process and equally freaked out at the side effects of a medicated birth. I attended two Lamaze classes and then dropped out after the instructor advised Dad to pinch Mom with increasing intensity as a way of simulating labor pains. Although I hadn't been through labor yet, I'd never heard it described as a pinch. My first delivery was hospital intervention at its best, and I gave birth to a healthy baby boy. Upon arriving home, the first order of business was to find loving homes for both dogs. I now knew the difference between pets and people, and my pets weren't ready for little people.

My next two deliveries were non-medicated, and it was then that I discovered nature's birth control. Nothing could have prepared me for that kind of pain. One of my babies was born perfectly healthy. One was born with a hole in his heart. Nothing could have prepared me for this either.

Life with a newborn was recognizable for the week that

mom or mother-in-law visited. She took care of everything, except feeding the baby. That was plenty for me. After she left, it was all me, all day at home. I balanced breastfeeding, body care, and baby with carpooling, homework, dinner, and after-school sports—not to mention laundry, bill paying, and grocery shopping. When I added colic, sleep deprivation, illness, breast infections, diaper rash, and ear infections to the mix, I became completely overwhelmed, lost, and frustrated. My husband was exceptionally helpful, but he traveled for work. There were more days and nights than I care to remember when I was alone with children, exhausted, and wondering if I'd made a horrible choice in deciding to become a mom. In my darkest hours, I remember sitting in the rocking chair trying to comfort a crying baby and finally sobbing myself until I had no energy left to cry.

When I did find a moment to think, my thoughts swirled around the inequities of motherhood. How was it that one woman was expected to take care of this little angel, herself, her family, and her home at the same time? How was I supposed to "sleep when the baby sleeps" when I was so behind on housework? Why didn't anybody tell me about the personal holocaust that accompanies motherhood? Here's a journal entry I wrote just after my third child was born:

January 19

I wish I could impart my new respect for the conse-
quences of intercourse to the 16-year-old girls I just
saw on the news who want to have babies now so they
can "be friends with their kids." Oh please.

I feel so alone. My husband NEVER gets overwhelmed, and this annoys me. I accuse him of being
unimpassioned about everything because of his clear
absence of emotional involvement. He says simply,
"What needs to get done will get done." Intellectually,
I know this, too. Now try telling it to my life. For me,
it simply doesn't happen like this. Everywhere I look in
the house I am reminded of things I need to do. Here's
what's on my list today: address birth announcements;
send birthday gifts to my niece and two nephews; pay
the bills; mail my sister's maternity clothes back along
with the open can of formula that she left during her
visit (it expires in three weeks); design birthday invita-
tions for my 3-year-old's party; update car insurance

with information on new mini-van; file warranties from Christmas gifts; label photos; buy a wedding gift for a couple that was married five months ago; buy four baby gifts; take my 11-year-old shopping to buy pants that are only available at Gap Kids; write thank-you notes from Christmas; put away Christmas wrapping; move computer back to its home on the Christmas wrapping table. There's more, but I'm too tired to write it down.

Other mothers nodded when I said that I was depressed, overwhelmed, exhausted, and didn't know what to do about it. Yet motherhood seemed to be a solitary rite of passage—at least in my culture. A few friends brought dinners by the house. Some offered to watch the baby for an hour or two. Others invited my older sons to their homes to give me some time. While I appreciated the offers for babysitting, I rarely took advantage of them. It seemed to be more of an effort to ready the baby for a sitter than it was to care for him myself. Also, I was uncomfortable asking for help from women who I assumed were busy with their own children. In my world, "busy" was synonymous with "overwhelmed." It didn't feel right to ask another overwhelmed mother to help me with my children.

I had decided to stay home "for the kids." Staying home was part of my Good Mom image. Central to this image were things like volunteering at school; being a Room Mom, Den Mom, or Team Mom; having a clean house; baking cookies; heading off summer boredom by filling the calendar with field trips, movies, crafts, picnics, beach days, campouts, and museum visits; throwing birthday parties with clever themes; having the kids' friends play at our house—with computer games, a trampoline, a tree house, a zip-line, remote-control cars, and all types of trendy toys; driving to extracurricular activities; decorating the kids' bedrooms; and shuttling for play dates.

There's more.

I also expected to stay in good physical condition, be bright and cheerful, and stay informed on current events. I expected economic success, a great marriage, and excellent health. Three babies later, I realized that I didn't actually know one person who embodied my image of a "Good Mom." Still, I clung to the idea that someday I would have it all pulled together. After all, the other moms I knew looked so together. If they could do it, so could I.

In pursuit of this Good Mom image, I went out of

balance. I began reacting rather than responding. My behavior was off-center, emotionally driven, and beyond what a situation called for. It was triggered by a variety of external stimuli: children, family, friends, neighbors, and the media. At the core was an exaggerated sense of self-importance. I was convinced that I knew what it took to be a Good Mom. However, while I was doing what it took, I was also losing my self-respect—mostly because I had no self to attach the respect to.

I felt very responsible for bringing three babies into this world, and I was now in a habit of putting all of my energy into their lives. I reasoned that I would have time for self-development and a life of my own "when the children were grown." This was my time to be a mom, and I was ALL MOM. My perspective was so warped at the time that when I met a woman who was traveling with a girlfriend rather than her husband, I assumed that she was having marital problems. The truth was that she and her husband simply enjoyed different types of vacations. At the time, I had no frame of reference for understanding a woman who was creating choices.

- CHAPTER 1 -

Mama Drama

MY FAIRY GODMOM SAYS, "HELL HAS A SPECIAL
PLACE FOR GUSHY WOMEN."

Do you know a gushy mom? She's emotional, hyper, and
overly enthusiastic. I feel uneasy around her because she
appears to be playing a role, rather than being herself. I call
it Mama Drama. My Fairy Godmom says it happens when a
woman acts on images of motherhood rather than on her
inherent intuition.

Such images are imposed upon us from the media, experts
of all kinds, well-meaning family members, and veteran
parents. Our values develop and are realized as we act on

those internal "clicks" we call intuition. When we observe the results as they pertain to our deep sense of well-being, we can learn more about living from the inside out.

Advertising is designed to elicit an emotional response to an image. When we try fulfilling these external images, we end up unfulfilled and wondering why we don't measure up. Whose yardstick are we using, anyway? However, as we identify our passions, we may become more aware of what truly matters to us day-by-day. Each of us is passionate about something. Imagine living our lives with the courage to make choices that support our satisfaction. Wow! Life now includes us as well as those we love.

When we get attached to images, there are two roles that we might decide to dramatize. One is the "Take-Charge Woman." Here, we deal with our emotions by doing everything on our own because no one else will get it right. Explaining something to someone else takes too much time. We give 100% and have no patience with what we perceive to be incompetence. Our children are overly dependent on us, and our husbands are probably hen-pecked. We claim that we can never find time for ourselves. Any warm-hearted soul that calmly suggests we "take some time away" risks being told that he/she "just doesn't understand how impossible that would be."

The other type is the "Go with the Flow Girl." Here, we attach ourselves to other people. We don't make plans until we check with everyone else. We put ourselves last if, in fact, we are on the list at all. We are certain that our mission on the planet is to help other people, whatever that means at the moment. We use the phrase "Are you sure?" time and again because we have lost touch with our natural confidence through too much self-sacrificing of our time and space. We assume that we know how others are feeling when we don't even know how we are feeling much of the time. We think of ourselves as "good girls." Our husbands are our heroes.

Many of us see these roles played out in our lives. So, what's the midpoint? The midpoint is found in honest moments—those in which we take a split second to determine what we need and want from the experience that's directly in front of us. By taking a split second for ourselves, we can continue to participate in whatever is going on while still allowing an internal pause to occur. When we ignore our need for this pause, it begins to feel much like a child who comes to you gleefully ready to share something and desperately wants your attention—Mom . . . Mom . . . Mom? . . . Mom! . . . MomMomMomMom . . . **MOM!!!** See how demanding the need becomes when we ignore it? It doesn't just go away, it increases. It keeps giving us pressure until we listen. Many times, we feel as though we don't have the attention to give to anyone or anything because we've ignored our own need for attention for so long. Have we considered that much of what we do for others might be for attention and isn't important to anyone, including us? If what we do is necessary, have we considered that how we are doing it might be draining our energy?

Allowing ourselves to notice these subtle yet important questions is as tricky as answering them, especially when we have been entrenched in doing things for others first, last, and always. One simple thing that we can do is to begin with something small—teeny tiny if you wish. "I wish I had a clean house." "I would love to have dinner cooked for me." "I want to travel to Spain." Begin with a small step that represents that desire to you. For example, take ten minutes to make one part of the house clean and beautiful—not a room, just a corner. If having dinner cooked would make you happy, consider buying part of your dinner, such as a main dish, a side dish, or even a loaf of fresh-baked bread. If you want to go to Spain, take a few minutes to get on the Internet or call a travel agent.

Society's image-making literally banks on us acting out images of motherhood. Instead, let's look for inspiration on the many ways there are to be a mom. Then we can choose what to accept with full awareness and what to replace with our own script for individual growth. For now, let's share a giggle over our Mama Drama behaviors and discover what triggers these reactions in each of us.

Needing Others More

Mama Drama is what happens when we need others to need us more than we need ourselves. I'll say it again in boldface: **Mama Drama is what happens when we need others to need us more than we need ourselves.** It's a shift that occurs when we become distracted from who we are by unconsciously deciding that we don't know enough to deal with what's in front of us. So, we focus our attention on something external: expert advice; good-mom images; religious, political, and economic doctrines and trends; or some other paradigm that tells us what to do and how to do it.

Below is a list of Mama Drama behaviors. The pronoun "she" is used to remind us of how often we see these behaviors in others before recognizing them in ourselves:

- She inserts herself into disagreements to which she is not a party.

- She arranges schedules for people who are capable of doing it themselves.

- She sets up play dates for children who are old enough to decide who they want to play with.

- She offers unsolicited advice to just about anyone.

- She often says "yes" when she needs to say "no" and is baffled as to why she has so little time to herself.

- She is overly involved in her children's performance. This goes for homework, club projects, sports, and social life. She has been known to turn down plans for a movie or a night out with friends because her child has a test to study for, a huge project due, or a lot of homework.

- She strives for *Good Mother Merit Badges*. Cookies and milk are great; however, Good Mother rituals done without regard for change or the flow of life eventually lose their luster. What was rooted in inspiration is now fed by (and eaten in) guilt.

- She uses the pronoun "we" instead of "they" when talking about her children. "We're teething." Enough said.

- She over-schedules her children. It's terrific to offer children a variety of activities that match their interests and energy. Remember though, many writers, musicians, and artists didn't develop a passion for their talent in after-school enrichment programs. They discovered it through periods of boredom, frustration, or anger.

- She gives her children what she did or didn't have as a child and expects her children to appreciate all she's doing for them in this upgraded version of her childhood.

- She believes she is indispensable.

- She is very outspoken about the standards she has for her children.

- Comments from her friends also tell us something. Here's one that she hears frequently: "You're so different when you're away from your kids." (If you unconsciously read this as "You're so different when you're away from your kids **and husband**," we need to talk!)

Mama Drama in Action

My Fairy Godmom called me recently with an example of Mama Drama that appeared in our local newspaper. A police officer spotted a Volvo station wagon speeding at 61 mph through a 45-mph area. The officer pulled the car over and prepared to write a citation. The driver, a mother with her 5-

year-old son, grabbed the officer's citation book and took off. She rolled several stop signs and, at one point in the chase, tossed the citation book out her window. The 10-minute chase ended at an elementary school, where the child was escorted to his classroom and his mother was escorted to jail. Apparently, the woman's husband had yelled at her about getting their child to kindergarten on time.

I was at the beach one day when another Mama Drama scenario unfolded nearby. Four children were busy building a sandcastle at the water's edge. An assortment of buckets and shovels were traded back and forth throughout the construction. David, who looked to be about five, caught my eye when he sneaked away from the group carrying a yellow bucket with raised patterns—ideal for sandcastle frieze.

David let out a clever laugh as he admired his take. He was leaving the sandcastle suburbs to build his dream castle. As he reveled in his accomplishment, sister Hannah, about eight, noticed the missing bucket. She spotted it near David and tiptoed up behind him. When she was close enough, she grabbed the yellow bucket on the run. She dashed down to the sandcastle group as David chased after her screaming for his bucket. With a good lead on her brother and apparently enjoying the attention, Hannah led the Hannah/bucket/David whiplash to where her parents were sunbathing. By this time, David was growling and frothing at the mouth.

Hannah stopped short, right in front of Mom and Dad. David arrived a second later and gave Hannah his best, open-handed slap on the back.

Dad's response: "Hey, what's going on with you two?"

Mom responded with the flexibility of a ninja as she jumped from prone position to fighting stance in one smooth move. David immediately recognized the threat and bolted. As David ran, Mom screamed after him, "David! David! You come back here right now or I'm taking you home!"

David's response: "No!"

At this point, I fully expected Mom to make good on her threat. Instead, she just stood there. Her fighting stance wilted into awkward defeat. David walked away, victorious. Mom sat down in a beach chair and went on conversing with friends as though nothing had happened. From what I could gather, Mom couldn't enforce the threat she levied. She and her family were at the beach with three other families, and she was unwilling or unable to leave just because David didn't obey her. Acting dramatically may have a place in life-or-death situations, but sharing toys is generally not life-threatening. How will children distinguish between what's life-or-death and what's not, if we react to everything as though it's life-or-death?

More Mama Drama

Here are a few more Mama Drama moves:

- She insists that doing something on her own is easier than accepting help because another person won't do it "right"—her way.

- She acts as the emotional rudder for those around her. When 4-year-old Junior opens a birthday gift at his party, she overdoes the moment by shrieking, "Oh Junior, isn't that cool!?" Then she writes thank-you notes in Junior's voice.

- She schedules her own activities, if any, after she finds out what everyone else is doing.

- She rarely accepts direct answers and will often reply, "Are you sure? I don't want to impose. Is that okay?" She's quite sure that she knows how others are feeling and what their motivations are—despite what they tell her.

- She does things for her children rather than with them. Once the children lose interest, she stops whatever it is because she's doing it for them.

– She treats her husband like a child. She instructs him on how to care for the children when she's away. She reminds him of all the details, because she knows he'll forget if she doesn't say something. (If she does this often enough, he gives up and does forget!)

In the end, she feels so responsible for everything that happens or doesn't happen in the family that she goes overboard. She has no boundaries. There's nothing she won't do for the so-called benefit of her children and family. They are the audience for her drama. And who will be her audience when they're no longer at home? Who knows? Maybe she'll never allow them to fully leave home because she'll need them as her audience. Maybe she'll find other people and places to act out her drama because the drama is inside of her. She's a drama queen and, for now, motherhood is her starring role.

Leaving the Stage

Once we recognize these behaviors in ourselves, we can then separate from them. From this point, we can begin to live our lives as women first and mothers also. There's a television advertisement for a pain reliever that shows a young mother with a child standing next to her. Emotionally charged phrases flash across the screen:

Help is NOT on the way . . .

You're on your own . . .

Deal with it . . .

As you can guess, the product is pitched as the kind of help every overwhelmed mom needs. It's true that healthy women ask for help but not from a pill. Here's how I found mine . . .

CHAPTER 2

Meeting My Fairy Godmom

IN 1988, I WAS THE MOTHER OF A 16-MONTH-OLD SON AND WORKING FULL-TIME AS AN OFFICE MANAGER.

Two months into my job, the owner of the company (William) offered me a consultation with a woman named Patrece. Patrece had established a non-profit educational corporation dedicated to preserving and updating ancient wisdoms. One way this is done is through the recognition of individual energy patterns. It was William's belief that the more people know specifically about themselves, the more effective they are in life: relationships, jobs, everything. I accepted the offer to meet with Patrece, but I had no idea what to expect.

On a warm August day, I met Patrece in her home overlooking the Pacific Ocean. While a fluffy white dog slept in the corner, Patrece explained that each of us is on the planet to learn a specific lesson. We are born with a unique energy pattern that brings to us the experiences we need to learn and grow. No two people have the same pattern, which means that the same experience can translate into something different for each of us. Choices figure into the equation, of course, and in every experience we have a choice between stagnation and growth.

Since that first meeting, many of our discussions have centered on my experience of raising children. Patrece is a generation ahead of me and has a daughter my age. I share my concerns, and she gently reminds me of what I already know. She offers a counterpoint to my exaggeration. What I appreciate so much is the in-depth and far-reaching nature of what she offers from her training and experience. She doesn't hand me solutions to problems. Instead, she points out the magical in the mundane.

Sometimes I argue. Sometimes I choose not to understand. But always, always I experiment with the information. Gradually, a shift occurs—first in me, then in my marriage and finally with my children and me. I never dreamed I could enjoy life as much as I do now.

The shortened version of Fairy Godmother to Fairy Godmom comes with good reason. She is as direct and concise as the shortened version of the word. One day, I phoned her to say that I would be unable to make a meeting that evening because I was sick. She knows my once-upon-a-time (now past) tendency to over-extend myself with family, friends, causes, and projects. While a Fairy Godmother might have sent me best wishes for getting well and a recipe for a medicinal tea, my Fairy Godmom said simply, "Julie, you already know what to do about that." This was the end of our conversation. I knew what was left unsaid. I found my essential oils, took a soothing lavender bath, and dressed for the meeting. Sometimes a good kick in the rear is the kindest way to remind me to act on what I know. Nowadays, I am able to catch myself in time. I don't have to use huge mood swings or full-blown illnesses to get my own attention. This delicious sense of empowerment beats any Mama Drama.

The statements and questions that follow are some of my own and some that I hear from other mothers. While we share many experiences and feelings as mothers, there is more that is different between us. My hope is that we will grow to appreciate our uniqueness as women first and mothers also. In doing so, we change the world by changing how we are in the world.

•   •   •

"Nobody told me it would be like this."

Admitting this to ourselves can be the beginning of our maturity from girls into women, provided we move beyond our Personal Pity Party. Why do we expect to be told about motherhood? Who owes us an explanation? When women share their experiences, do we truly believe that ours will be the same as another's? If motherhood is anything, it's a mystery. It begins as a mystery, hidden deep within us. Ours are the hidden ways from which we create. There are as many ways to be a mother as there are mothers to create those ways.

My sister-in-law is seven months pregnant with her first child and the doctor recently ordered bed rest. She's frustrated because she feels fine, but she's having symptoms that mean something different to her doctor. "Nobody told me [pregnancy] would be this bad," she says to me over the phone. She asks about my labor and delivery experience, and I share parts of it with her. I'm ambivalent about sharing the pain of natural childbirth, but I want to be truthful.

She says that she's heard, "it's not that hard because of medication." She says that she's scared of the medication.

"I understand," I say. "I was too. Childbirth, for me though, turned out to be a worthwhile kind of pain."

She says that her mother had to have an emergency C-section with her first baby.

"What did your mom do then? Did she stop having kids?" I ask.

"No," said my sister-in-law. "She had me."

Later, I sent her this note:

When women share their birthing and parenting stories, your feeling of "there's something they're not telling me" is accurate. It's because we can't tell you the whole story. It would be like trying to tell you ahead of time what your wedding day will be like. When you listen to others' experiences, do you notice how certain parts resonate with you and other parts are forgotten? You've been pregnant for 7+ months now. How accurately can you describe what it's like to a friend who's never been pregnant? We women are mysterious creatures, and we like it that way. You're

going to experience birth in the same way that you've
experienced pregnancy: surrounding yourself with sup-
portive people, trusting your intuition, and being able
to laugh at yourself every so often.

My Fairy Godmom reminds me that, "We can't tell you what it's like, nor should we. Because if I tell you that this is the way it is and you believe me, then you'll have my experience, not your own. You may have fears and concerns, but which part of you do you wish to nurture? All you need are your abilities to listen and to choose.

"What can we offer a woman who is anxious and nervous about pregnancy and childbirth? I can't offer her what she's looking for, and she can't get from me what she thinks she needs. That's because of the mystery of being a woman. Let's consider enjoying the magical parts that come from allowing intrigue to exist. There are some things that cannot be explained. Have you noticed when we touch upon those 'things' and try to give explanations that foolishness reigns? That's when we must simply listen. It's the wise person who said, 'Think twice. Speak once.' The longer I live, the more I would like to add, 'Speak once, if at all.' Remember how we've talked about maturity as a willingness to allow space for ambiguity? We can listen to one another. We can share our presence and value one another's experience.

"Is a pregnant woman listening to anyone? The questions she asks are very different from what she really wants to know. 'Am I going to be safe?' 'Is the baby going to be healthy?' You can reassure her that our bodies are designed for this. It's all make-believe until your body is going through it. It's like when men think of war as though they're going to be heroes. Then they get into the battle. It's very different than their image. It's a life-altering experience.

"One of the wonders as we grow is to learn the dignity of holding our own counsel. There are things we just don't say because we love. We're creating an atmosphere from our attitudes."

"How do I get my life back?"

If we moms share anything, it's the experience of change. Some of us embrace our changing bodies. Others are repulsed. Some embrace the demands of babies. Others are overwhelmed. Some take sheer delight in the moment-to-moment unfolding of their mothering life. Others need organization and structure to feel comfortable. One thing many of us realize soon after giving birth is this: Giving birth doesn't make you a mom.

After I had my first child, I truly believed that I'd be the same person I'd been before, only now with a child in tow. Adding Junior to my juggling act didn't really work though. My Fairy Godmom calls it, "Extending a role beyond its time. Picture an 80-year-old woman dressing like a teenybopper. You've changed. Let yourself play catch-up." I know how I feel around a woman who has had a child but is determined not to change. There's a feeling that she's pretending about how her life truly is now.

My Fairy Godmom reminds me to, "Give yourself to the first three months. Allow and admit that you're not the person you were before the baby was born and that you won't be again; and that you don't even want to be. The choice to have a child has permanently changed your life. This is an in-between time from where you were to where you are going. You can't go back to who you (think) you were.

"When you allow yourself to become a mother and think of that as growing into and creating a new self, you have a much easier time. You don't come from a place of expectation and demand; rather, you focus more on observation and intuition. In developing awareness, you find confidence. Part of the frustration of the first few weeks or months is that you're trying to be a mother as your former self. That girl is gone. She is a woman now and has the choice of growing into a mother or not."

I used to work hard at being a mom. Too often, I would hear myself barking out orders like a drill sergeant. This usually happened when we had to be someplace at a specific time. For me, getting three children out the door with all the proper equipment seemed insurmountable.

We live two miles from the beach. At first, I blamed not going to the beach on our recent move. We were getting settled, I told myself, and didn't have all of our beach stuff in one place. What was truly keeping me from going to the beach was the Herculean effort it would take to gather the beach gear, load it into the car, get the kids into the car, park the car, and then get the kids and the stuff from the car to the beach with minimal help. One trip to the beach required bathing suits, towels, playpen (for baby's nap), body board and fins, sand toys, beach chair, ice chest (with nutritious, homemade lunch), sunscreen, drinking water, and hats. My thinking was that if I was going to go to all this "trouble," then we were going to make it "worth the effort" by staying for a while. That's where I was wrong. We didn't have to stay for a long time. The kids just wanted to go to the beach.

I was using my mother-of-one approach in a mother-of-three experience. As a mother of one, I had fewer items to bring to the beach and I could stay as long as my one child was comfortable. As a mother of three, I have more stuff to bring and more factors in the comfort equation. Growing into being a mother of three has meant that I am less attached to outcomes and more aware of doing things for as long as they are enjoyable.

"She makes it look so easy. She looks so together."

She doesn't spend enough time with her children. *She* spends too much time with her children. *She* doesn't need to work. *She* is so clever, creative, and smart. *She* is always put-together. *She* has a clean house. *She* has a nanny. *She* has a husband who helps with the children. *She* is having an affair. *She* volunteers for everything. *She* is never home. *She* is in great shape. *She* doesn't even know where her children are. *She* is a control freak. *She* had her nose, boobs, stomach, rear end, legs, eyes, or face fixed. *She* colors her hair.

Notice that when you read each statement, a different woman comes to mind, proving once and for all that *She* doesn't exist. *She* is a reflection of us. *She* helps us identify what matters most to each of us. Criticism is the most popular form of Mama Drama. The lion's share of criticism takes root when we pay more attention to images and concepts and less to our internal truth buttons.

My Fairy Godmom reminds me that, "More often than not, people show us only what they want us to see and tell us only what they want us to hear. We then insist on making comparisons with other mothers, their children, and their lifestyles. We have come to call this 'civilized living.' However, let's not tire ourselves into believing that we know enough about another to judge who is better than and who is less than. We are just getting to know our own mothering ways. We don't know for others. Humbling, isn't it?"

When we have a strong emotional response to the choices that other mothers are making, we must take a moment and unravel what's behind the strong emotion. I ask myself, "What's missing in my own life that makes me feel threatened by the choices she is making for herself?" My trigger is happy, working moms who don't need to work for financial reasons. And guess what? During the writing of this book, I became a happy, working mother who didn't write for financial reasons. If you're envious because She has the money to hire a nanny or She has a housekeeper, then position yourself to do the same—even if it's on a small scale. Do whatever it takes to stop thinking that someone else is living out your dreams.

Were we to address our passions, we might be more sensitive to the individual growth cycles that are constantly occurring. Perhaps we're lacking confidence in the areas in which we judge others most harshly. Or, maybe we haven't identified what passionate living feels like and looks like for ourselves. Therefore, we spend valuable time and energy focusing on others.

At one time, I was way too focused on people's cars. I couldn't understand why some people drove beat-up, old cars. *(Can we take a moment to praise growth? I can't believe I used to think like this!)* All these cars needed, in my opinion, was some bodywork and paint. In some cases, a good car wash would have helped. Here is how life gently addressed my oh-so-shallow confusion:

In 1991, I was a single parent and had to sell my Volvo because I couldn't afford to fix the clutch. For transportation, my grandmother graciously gave me her car because she was no longer driving. I became the proud owner of a 1979 Mercury Monarch. The car was twelve years old and had 19,000 miles on it. (That's less than 1,600 miles a year.)

The Monarch was duct-tape gray with a perfect coffin-red interior, except for the ashtray. Granny was a chain-smoker. I drove with the windows down for months. The car's exterior was another story. The last three letters were missing from the car's model name, which was written across the trunk. Instead of "Monarch," it just said "Mona." Mona's crowning feature was a collection of deeply rusted holes on the hood, the roof, and the trunk—all the unfortunate result of coastal living. The pattern of holes resembled huge, rusted bird droppings. Friends and acquaintances offered well-intentioned advice on giving Mona a makeover.

"Go to the junkyard for parts," one said.

"Buy a used hood for the car," said another.

"Go down to Earl Scheib and get it painted for $99 or paint it yourself," said others.

None of this advice made sense to me. I didn't have the money, and the car needed a lot of work. One day, a neighbor came up with an idea that appealed to my ecological side and my budget. She suggested that I crunch up empty beer cans, shove them into the rusted holes and cover them with duct tape. Mona was the color of duct tape anyway. What damage could I do?

Several weeks later, I got the answer to my question. I was on the freeway when I noticed duct tape flapping around on the hood. Within minutes, it flew off, and crushed beer cans littered the highway. After that, I realized that Mona was just basic transportation, so why should I put any more time or money into her? This was a simple truth, but one I couldn't grasp until I was living it.

When I am tempted to criticize, I remember that I am seeing only a slice of another person's life. I certainly wouldn't want to be evaluated by some of my own slices. Behind my need to criticize, I often discover confusion. When I'm confused, it's tempting to focus on something outside of myself. It's then that life grants me a similar circumstance so that I may gain perspective.

"I don't like being a mom as much as I thought I would. Sometimes I think maybe I shouldn't have had children."

For some moms, negative feelings and motherhood are mutually exclusive. For others, they are mutually confusing. In either case, they are rarely accepted as compatible. Says one mom, "It feels good just to be able to express the feelings of not always enjoying motherhood. I remember going to those play groups when Betsy was a toddler and feeling so lonesome because everyone just talked about how great it all was. No one ever brought up the difficulties. I feel like there are a lot of ways to be a mother."

I used to worry about the effect that my negative feelings might have on my children. I worried that they would feel unloved and that I would be labeled "selfish" or "whiny." The guilt associated with negative feelings is so strong for some women that they adopt a Pollyanna perspective. If negative feelings are shared, they're immediately followed with a positive spin. One way women control other women is through exclusion and isolation. Stuffed, negative feelings can be very isolating, especially to one's self.

Says another mom, "Motherhood is demanding, but I understand from parents with older children that this is a time to cherish. I'm ambivalent about not fully enjoying motherhood. I've been told that my husband and I are in the 'Golden Years of Childhood' when there's no one in diapers and no one driving. I want to appreciate this time, but I find myself dreaming of getting my life back. I imagine what my life will look like when the children are grown—just like I imagined my life with children before I had them."

My Fairy Godmom reminds me that, "Life is *not* a dress rehearsal. We make our choices, and we live the real life. As the current commercial says, 'Having a baby changes everything.' Allow the changes to occur. The point of any experience is to cycle through it and integrate what you need from it. You wanted the children. Then you had them, and then you think, 'Oh what if I hadn't had them?' You would've missed the experience. I don't know one parent, even if they say they wish they had not had children, who would have missed the experience. They *know* because they have had the experience. Although they think they would not have wanted it, the truth is they did not want to go on without the experience of having children. They wanted it. Do you really believe that you would have been the same person even **without** children? We all change."

"How can someone make an intellectual decision about an experience?" I ask.

"We can't make an intellectual decision about any experience. We have experiences, and our intellect analyzes," my Fairy Godmom replies. "The 'ticking clock' in a woman is that she wants the experience now. Her body is ready. She is saying, 'This is what I want now.'"

As adults looking back at our upbringing, we sometimes view our parents as good or bad, rather than a bit of both. As parents, something we can always share with our children is to be authentic human beings. Our children need us, as parents, to live as true to ourselves as possible. We need that from ourselves as well. When that occurs, children know that they can say something and we won't take it personally. Children sense a certain confidence of well-being that comes from that unspoken place. From Day One, children are observing us. They are learning to survive by trusting what they feel is acceptable or unacceptable, as much as by what they are being "taught." Authenticity happens moment-by-moment as we give our love and attention to what truly matters.

Write down the advantages there are for you in being a mom and tuck your list somewhere in this book. Here are some that inspire me: cuddling and rocking my baby; putting my nose and lips to a warm, fuzzy head; appreciating quiet moments; seeing newness every day; hearing scrambled words ("my ties are unshoed"); and realizing that everyone is someone else's baby. Now it's your turn.

"I can't handle staying home with my kids."

While I am more confident as the years go by, I have never felt like I'm "handling it" at home. The demands shift from sheer physical demands to more emotional and mental ones. I tried returning to part-time work but couldn't escape the feeling that I was missing something by being away from home so frequently. There were qualities that I saw in other women who were mothers and grandmothers that I wanted to develop in myself. Staying home with my children was my way to do this.

As I write this, my boys are 16, 8, and 4 and I am "living for kindergarten." By the time my youngest starts kindergarten, my oldest will be a senior in high school. This will be the first time that all three of my children are in school at the same time. This is when I will finally take time for myself. This is when I will exercise regularly, keep the house clean, and finish all those projects I've started. This is when I will read that stack of books I've had to pass up, and I'll finally return to writing.

But I know better.

This isn't how it will be—especially if I spend my HERE wishing for THERE. I am discovering that if I spend HERE wishing for THERE, THERE may never happen as I am imagining it HERE. If I can't be HERE NOW, how will I ever be THERE THEN? My desire for time to myself is something that I want NOW. If I don't act on this desire now, it will continue to demand my attention in irritating ways until I take some small action to let myself know that I'm listening to me.

I'm uncomfortable about hiring a babysitter for a few hours a week. It means adding to an already tight budget. It means interviewing strangers and hiring someone that I'm not completely sure of to watch my children. I decide it's safer and easier to wait until my youngest goes to kindergarten. This lets me dream about how great a mom I'll be when I have things my way. Plus, I have a handy excuse for all my other problems.

But what about my perfect future? If any of the following (very plausible) scenarios takes shape down the road, then I'll still have someone to care for:

- I could become pregnant again.
- My oldest son could present me with a grandchild way too early.
- A relative or friend could pass over, and I could end up caring for their child(ren).
- An aging parent could contract a debilitating disease and make the same demands on me that a young child might.

All these and more are possibilities. My challenge is to establish time for myself with the terms that exist right now. My spirit is nudging me to make small changes in the direction that I want to go. Perhaps a high school girl could help me out in the afternoon. Maybe my sister and I could trade one morning a week of babysitting. Heck, I could go to bed a little earlier and get up before my family. Whatever solution I try, the important part is that I am addressing my desire now and not waiting for more ideal circumstances to unfold.

But I'm not there yet. I insist on becoming frustrated by telling myself that I am doing the right thing for the children. And slowly, I grow more resentful and more critical of mothers who take any time for themselves. I go out of balance and into Mama Drama. I want someone to recognize the sacrifices that I am making for my children. Sacrifices are those things I do but don't really enjoy. And yet, something inside of me is fed by martyrdom. I insist on acting angry and overwhelmed. I insist on ignoring the small voice inside that says just take one small step in the right direction and see what happens. I ignore that voice until I am so wiped out that I'm crying daily and hating my life as a stay-at-home mom.

Finally, I take a small step and tell a close friend that I am looking for help with my children. I am richly rewarded for an ounce of courage. My girlfriend can't believe that she's never mentioned "Cassie," her favorite babysitter. I call Cassie and she turns out to be an ideal match. She arrives at my door, and her enthusiasm washes over my boys. They are so taken with her that they barely wave goodbye as I leave.

At first, I spend time on healthcare appointments. Then, I get a haircut. A few weeks later, I spend a little time at the library to write. Finally, I take it to the limit: I work in my home studio while Cassie plays with the boys downstairs. I write for four hours!

When I take time for myself while being a stay-at-home mom, I have a sense of personal well-being. I have an arrangement that I know works well for my family and me, and I have no interest in criticizing other moms. I find that if I'm content in what I'm doing and how I'm being, there's no need for external recognition, and there's no sense of sacrifice. Most importantly, I am present. My perfect future has no hold on me because I'm too busy with now.

"I have never gotten my figure back after having a baby."

My Fairy Godmom reminds me that pregnancy pulls us out of shape. "When you're pulled out of shape, as in pregnancy, you're taking what you have—your body—and you're making something different with it now. Another way to think of it is, once you know something, you can't not know it—and so it is with your body. Once you've had a baby, you can't go back to not having a baby. It's just like everything else in life. When you know, you look at others and say, 'Wow! That's how it was then.' Many things happen when you're pregnant."

My pregnant sister-in-law asked me about stretch marks and tanning her tummy. I said, "I have some stretch marks, but I didn't think about them until you just brought it up. For me, it hasn't been a big deal. I used to be able to sit in a beach chair with no wrinkles in my tummy, and now I have wrinkles."

My Fairy Godmom added, "You see? One day it's important and the next day it's not. I think that pregnant women who keep journals will find it most interesting. Your hormones get very bossy. And remember, it's not just pregnancy that has changed you. I know a lot of child-free women who are not at all like they were four or five years ago. Change happens."

One day, my 12-year-old and I were unpacking dishes after their weeklong stay in moving boxes. We had washed the first load in the dishwasher, and they were ready to be put away. As my son reached for a plate, he said, "Mom, where do the plates go?"

"I don't know Jake. I haven't lived here before," I replied.

"Mom! Come on! Where do the plates go?"

"I don't know." I said. "Where do you think they should go?" Exasperated, he opened a few cupboards, found an empty one, and started putting away the dishes. Change happens.

"I want more time alone."

My Fairy Godmom reminds me that, "Wanting more time alone can also mean a need for privacy. Do you want more time alone or just more privacy? Sometimes it can mean, 'I want to be alone with my family.' You can have privacy together. You can allow your family to be alone with you. Privacy doesn't have to be time and space away. You can do things next to each other. We as women are well-qualified to establish this for our families and ourselves.

"What invades your privacy? Telephone? TV? Radio? Traffic noise? When we start identifying the stimulus that invades our privacy and we eliminate it, we can create more space—even with others around. Remember, self-talk invades our space, and some of that can be noisier than children demanding attention."

My two younger boys share a small bedroom so that the fourth bedroom in our home can serve as my writing studio. Each boy has a wooden cigar box hidden somewhere in the room, and it's understood that the box is only for its owner to open. Their nightstands and beds are private spaces as well. When I moved past my image that each boy should have his own room, I realized that the boys actually like sharing a room. For a while, they pushed their single beds together, and we spent many evenings sprawled out on the double bed reading books and talking before bedtime.

Perhaps the first step toward privacy is recognizing the moments that do belong to you. Maybe you only have a few seconds to yourself right now, but practice being aware and using what little time you do have for your own benefit. Take a moment to focus on what you love about yourself and the new things you're doing as a mom that you never dreamed would be a part of your life. When you increase your ability to pay attention, you expand on the emerging qualities that you are finding out about yourself.

If you find yourself in limbo just waiting until the next person needs you, be aware of it. You've just discovered your first moment to yourself. No one needs you this very moment. My Fairy Godmom reminds me that, "First, we discover moments. These overflow into hours where we understand that no one needs our total attention and active participation. We get to see that maybe it was our need to be needed that kept us so very busy."

What makes you happy? A catnap? A cup of tea? Having help at home? For me, it's an uninterrupted moment to enjoy the flow of my own thoughts. The more we claim these mini-moments, the more moments we have. It's called creating time. Let's learn to be less involved when and where it isn't necessary. Let's keep our fingers on those activities that give us satisfaction until we naturally accept that pleasure is permissible.

**"I want to give my kids what I didn't have.
I want them to have the best of everything."**

Okay, so your childhood wasn't as stellar as someone else's. It happens. Maybe your mom worked, so now you've decided to stay home with your children. Maybe you work now because your mom stayed home. While you were growing up, were you aware that your parents were giving you what they never had as children?

As adults, our children will decide—independent of what we've done for them—whether or not they had a so-called "good childhood." Over the course of their lives, they may even change their minds on this issue several times. Rather than giving our children what we never had, let's make an effort to give ourselves what we need now to be happy parents.

Some parents act out of a self-centeredness that is masked by the nobility of caring for one's own and doing good for others. My Fairy Godmom reminds me that, "We go to great lengths to fill time and space for our children as if we need to pour into an empty vessel. Observe, observe, and observe some more. There is an authentic human being emerging right there in front of us at all times. If we do everything for these little companions, we give the message: 'You cannot do this. I have to do it for you. You cannot answer that question. I must answer it for you.' Over time, this becomes true [and boring]. At every phrase of their development and ours, we're offering our children an example. As parents, this is our **real** job."

"I want to be a good role model for my children."

I hear some moms say things like, "I'm proud of the fact that I work for my son's/daughter's sake." These moms say that it's important to show their children that a woman can do more than just be a stay-at-home mom. My Fairy Godmom reminds me that, "There's no such thing as a role model because there's never been you before, and there will never be this you again.

"When we do something to get a reaction, it's manipulative. We're role-playing. When we role-play as moms, we raise children who role-play. They feel one way but act another. Everyone gets mixed messages. We can be an inspiration to our children, but having the intention of being a role model is a subtle difference. A role model is making choices because of how those choices will look to another. Each day, we face new ways of being. We can exemplify a quality or a way of being, but there are no guarantees that how we are or what we do will impact our children in the way that we expect."

There's a story that tells of a little boy who goes downstairs one morning and sees his mom. He says, "Mommy, you're beautiful!" This puzzles his mom because she's usually dressed for work in high heels, a suit, and wearing make-up. This particular morning, she is dressed in jeans and a sweater.

"Why do you say that when I'm dressed in jeans and a sweater?" she asks her son.

"Because," he replies, "when you're dressed like that I know you're going to be with me."

"I want to get my children a pet. I think it's good for children to learn about animals."

When I was a child, we had dogs, cats, a snake, a rat, bunnies, pigs, and a lamb over a span of thirteen years. The only pet I remember taking care of was a dwarf bunny that I hid in my closet for two weeks. Otherwise, the pets were family pets. As such, Mom took care of them.

I want my children to enjoy having pets. I want them to learn about animals. I want a dog, but I have a gerbil-sized yard. My boys say that they would rather have a trampoline than a dog. I suggest that we get a dog and name it "Tramp" so they can tell their friends they have a tramp at home. They don't think this is funny.

I ask my Fairy Godmom about this. I want my children to know what it's like to own a pet, but I understand very clearly who will be caring for it. How do I know that I'm doing this for the right reasons?

My Fairy Godmom replies, "How do you not know? We have to try hard not to know. Whenever you think to yourself 'How do I know?', ask yourself, 'How could I not know?' You really do know, and you must stop acting helpless. The whole idea is that we don't want to admit we know because then we think we're going to be responsible, and we don't want to be responsible for one more thing. The definition that I use for 'responsibility' is 'response to my own ability.' Let's take away the burden part of responsibility. There isn't a burden in being responsible unless we're being responsible for someone else, and how can you possibly respond as someone else— even your children?"

When I talk with people who own pets, my image gets shattered pretty quickly. These folks aren't living my image of pet ownership. To ignore what they're telling me about their experience is to pretend that I don't know. My Fairy Godmom reminds me that, "Acting on what you do know is going to lead you to discover what you don't know. If you say, 'I don't know,' identify what you do know and act from there.

If you say, 'I don't know,' there's a tendency to reach outside yourself for the answer. I want you to look inside for the answer. Do you have space in your life for something more? If you're looking for more time and space for yourself, then why fill it up with more of anything, pets included, for now?"

"We need a larger house, a bigger car, more money, etc."

We NEED more room, I say. We NEED a larger kitchen. We NEED a bedroom for each child. We NEED a guest room for grandparents. We NEED space for two home offices. We NEED a larger backyard. Basically, what we NEED is a mini-plantation or a starter castle. The more energy I put into looking for my dream house, the more frustrated I become. Housing prices have skyrocketed so much that I can't afford my own neighborhood. Two years ago, we put an offer on a fixer around the corner. It was a feng-shui nightmare and needed major remodeling. When I saw it for the first time, I was giddy with home improvement ideas. When my husband saw it for the first time, he stopped breathing.

My sister-in-law reminded me of how fortunate we are to own a home in Southern California. I know she's right. Even though it feels small and looks like every fourth house on the block, I'm discovering how much more relaxed I am when I operate from a base of stability. This house is walking distance to the boys' schools, and there are at least six children playing outside at any given time. Even groups of teenagers have been seen hanging around here.

Sure, we could use more space, but that might mean that I see my teenager and his friends less frequently. Sure, a guest room would be nice, but I know that I am happiest when there are spaces in my togetherness with family and friends. A larger backyard would be great, but my boys prefer to play in front of the house where their friends are. And working at home? My husband and I have tried every possible combination, and we end up with the same result each time: When he works at home, the focus shifts to keeping distractions and loud noises to a minimum. It feels more like we're living in his office and less like it's beneficial to have him working at home.

I know that a lot of time and energy will go into buying another house. We'll need to list ours for sale (keep it clean for realtors to show), pack our stuff, move it, and fix up the new place so it feels like home. This is the same time and energy that I now use to listen to myself, be with family and friends, laugh, enjoy the outdoors, and even . . . sometimes . . . waste a little bit of it. I'm unwilling to give up the quality of self that this house allows me.

My Fairy Godmom asks, "Do you need money and all that it can buy and buy and buy? Spending time buys more than we may ever need."

"People just don't understand. They don't have my kids."

This is absolutely right. It's fall here and local merchants are displaying artwork done by elementary school students. I've never seen so many styles, shapes, and colors of pumpkins! It reminds me that there isn't a right or wrong way to draw a pumpkin. Likewise, there isn't a right or wrong way to be a mom. In fact, why don't you draw a picture of a mom and send it to us? (See *Contact Us* for the address.) Maybe we'll hang them in store windows on Mother's Day.

The point is that Mama Drama begins when we are sure that there is a specific and right way to be a mom. Our Pity Party starts when we decide that no one understands what we are going through because we are not getting what we expected, wanted, or needed. In children, we call this type of behavior a tantrum. In ourselves, we feel that similar behavior is justified and is our right because of our Good Mom image.

My Fairy Godmom asks, "Why put so much energy into getting people to understand? Refer to the list you made earlier about the advantages of being a mom. You were clear and calm when you made that list. What changed? Did the terms let you down? Did someone or something get in the way of how you thought it should, could, or might be? If the exact same thing works again today and still again tomorrow and the next day, we will all be sleepwalking rather than being wide-awake, vital human beings. Change is inconvenient!"

"I want to give back for all that I've been given."

When I hear this, I think of when my son needed blood donations for open-heart surgery. I remember announcing to anyone who would listen that I am a life-long blood donor, and I encouraged everyone to be a life-long blood donor because of my experience. My Fairy Godmom reminds me that when I encourage others to act because of my experience, I not only shift my focus from myself to another, but I am also trying to make someone else grateful for my experience. We can't trade skins. We can't base our needs and wants on the experiences of others. We don't know the complexity of their experiences. (By the way, have you donated blood lately?)

My Fairy Godmom says, "Giving something because you believe that you are Mother Bountiful and these poor people don't have as much as you is to elevate yourself and discount others. If your intent is to 'take care of those who are less fortunate than you,' it's time to reconsider. Each of us is designed to take care of ourselves. When push comes to shove, we find ways to do exactly that with the hope that this brings out the best in each of us. The essence of giving is not about sacrifice. Sacrificing indicates a depletion, a going without. What does it mean if a mom believes she is sacrificing herself for her children? Does it mean that she doesn't have what she is giving? Then where does her gift come from? Nonsense. Such attitudes don't mean anything unless she is bargaining for the future. Her intention might be, 'Look at all I did for you when you were little and now that I am old, I need you.' All of us have heard this message inferred, if not stated, in one way or another, but it has nothing to do with the essence of giving. It's bargaining and deal-making. How do I know this? Because when something is truly given, it issues forth from a place that is never depleted. To give the gift of time, space, or diamonds is all part of the natural cycle of living. You can check this out for yourself. Watch how Mother Nature does it. There is always more."

Holiday gift giving offered me fertile ground for learning this one. I used to scour the stores to find unique gifts to please others. I would go to great lengths in hopes of a desired response from the recipient of my gift. This year, my 8-year-old reminded me of a different side of giving. He wanted to buy his younger brother a blow-up punching bag. He was so excited to give this gift that he wasn't the least bit disappointed when his younger brother didn't receive it with the same enthusiasm. For him, giving the gift completed his experience.

This year, my Fairy Godmom's favorite gift was a handwritten thank-you note she received from a man in his early forties who is just learning how to write. The time and emotional energy he dedicated to sitting down and trusting himself to find simple words that he could spell was a gift that her heart easily received and now treasures.

During the 2003 wildfires in California, I woke up one morning, went downstairs, and cut open an orange. It tasted so good and flushed out the smell and taste of smoke that had been in the air for days. I wanted to offer this experience to folks who had been evacuated to local shelters. The boys and I rounded up a few items that we were ready to pass along and stopped by the healthy food store to pick up a case of organic oranges. Ironically, the oranges had been harvested from a local farm that was now threatened by the fires.

As I was heading for the nearest shelter, my husband called and said that the Red Cross was advising people to drop off donations at one central shelter downtown. Hmmm. I understood the logic, but this wasn't part of how I wanted to participate. The downtown shelter was much farther than I intended to go that day, and the air quality was so bad that schools were closed. It was inadvisable to be out unless you absolutely had to. I knew what I wanted to do, but I gave in and dutifully drove my donation downtown. Signs scrawled on cardboard directed me to a back alley where a warehouse stood. Three men descended on my trunk like vultures. One wrote out a receipt for my donation, and we left. The boys didn't even get out of the car.

I came home disappointed because this wasn't the experience that I had wanted. I had given into outside influences that urged me to give from gratitude and guilt rather than from creativity. The conditions under which I gave varied from how I wanted to share. Most likely, the items were accepted and used as I intended. The point for me, however, is to continually find *inspiring* ways to get the job done—whatever that may be. I know it's possible.

"I want more time alone with my husband."

For many women, there's a feeling of wanting to go back to "the way we were." We see young couples and think of the time that we were young and in love. My Fairy Godmom reminds me that, "Going back to 'the way we were' is an image. We can't go back any more than young couples can advance forward to where we are now. Just as you were pulled out of shape physically with pregnancy, let love take on a new shape as well. There are many aspects to love. As they say, 'A hungry shopper isn't a good shopper.' And so it is with the eagerness and demands in a woman who wants more time with her husband. You cannot tell me that there isn't some humor stored within every event, especially when children are involved. Look at the world through the eyes and ears of your children for just a few minutes every day. I am told that once we have survived the first few weeks of life, we are convinced that we will survive. Now it's refinement time. What is refinement to you? To me, it definitely includes an appreciation for the unexpected. If we insist on role-playing, let's at least improvise. Use the moments as creative tools. Our children do. Stop. Look. Listen.

"Write down what feminine means to you. Do it quickly and before you read any further.

"See if the soft, kind, and gentle ways are qualities that you consider less than intelligent. How about 'discipline?' Did you include that word? Did you know that it is derived from 'disciple?' What we are dedicated to allows each of us to be naturally disciplined. It's the dedication that allows us to follow what matters most at each stage of our lives. Don't you find that the effort goes out of discipline when considered through the looking glass of willing participation? Each of us is born with an aspect of femininity that's never been on the planet before and never will be again. How is it that we get educated out of ourselves? Isn't it about time to unlearn what we have accepted that is now unacceptable to us? Play with the following statements and see where the fun takes you:

- I have accepted . . .
- I will not accept . . .
- I want to accept . . .

"What do you want to share with your husband? Conversational time? Romantic time? Jogging time? Your husband is waiting, watching, and hoping for you to be all that you can be. You see, he isn't a woman. Oh, you noticed—thank goodness! Once you truly recognize what a special presence you are, atmosphere follows."

I remember being part of a woman's group in which we met at each other's homes for dinner once a month. I was so inspired by how each woman hosted the gathering in her way. I discovered the pleasures of soft music, candles, and comfortable seating. My Fairy Godmom says, "Set an atmosphere, not an image. This is an important distinction. When you see somebody doing what you like, that's a point of reflection for you. That's within you. Just as when you see somebody doing something that you don't like, you know that's also a part of you or it would not register within you. We learn a lot through reflection, as we use the world for our mirror. You see, if it isn't in you, there isn't a point of reflection. You truly don't see it. Nothing registers."

There are as many ways to be a woman as there are women to create those ways. We are a reflection of nature in all of her diversity, abundance, beauty, and strength.

"I'm not interested in sex."

I used to think of sex as just one more thing that someone needed from me. After a day of doing things for the children, I needed to do something for myself. Crawling into bed and going to sleep was just fine, thank you. Forget about a private, intimate moment with my husband. I needed a moment alone.

My Fairy Godmom asks, "If sex feels like just one more thing that someone needs from you, what's one more thing that you need from yourself? How did you spend your day? Were you at all aware of moments during the day when it was safe to feel? We are so very over-stimulated. What does it mean to be a sensual person? It means something different to everybody."

"But, we're conditioned to think of sex in a masculine way," I say.

"Even if we think about sex in a feminine way, there may not be the energy of desire. Thoughts are thoughts and feelings are feelings. They come from two very different places. To think is not to feel. 'How can I fit sex into this evening?' is a thought. 'I don't feel like sex' is a thought. 'I don't want sex' is a thought. You tell me that there are days that you don't even want you, let alone sex. I laugh. I understand.

"Desire is such a delicious word. It spills over into everything in life. Imagine losing your taste buds and your desire for wonderful food. Boring! Imagine losing your desire to feel the sun on your skin or resisting the smell of freshly baked bread. It takes a lot of energy to turn off natural delights. What are you resisting? Is it, 'I don't want to feel; I am too busy thinking?' Thoughts come and go quickly. True feelings linger much longer. Then you may say, 'I don't have that kind of time.' If we were meant to think more than we were meant to feel, we would all be walking around with huge heads and little bodies.

"Since we are speaking about bodies, loving yours is a silent, undercover job that only you can do. Here we go again, back to the mystery of being a woman. Too much talk, too much thinking about the topic of sex has taken the enjoyment out of the hearts of women. An intimate partner once confided in me that he found great pleasure in being with a woman who was relaxed about being a woman. He said women who try to be what a man wants or pretend to be what a man wants can make a man feel like he's in a business deal or a power struggle, rather than having a meaningful experience. This is definitely different from the messages that are making sex a topic of concern in our society."

I say to my Fairy Godmom, "I used to expect my husband to just know certain things about me. Even when I didn't know these things about myself, I expected him to know about me just because . . ."

"Because a man should make you feel feminine?" she asks.

"Yes," I say.

She laughs and asks, "Has it worked? If you're demanding that a man should make you feel feminine, is that working for you? I doubt it. It's how you live your life. There are four basic needs: food, shelter, sleep, and sex. Sex is natural! Ask yourself, 'How much of my day is natural?' How many ways can you nurture yourself during the day so that you desire to share yourself, be enjoyed, and have pleasure? Are you the kind of person who wants sex once in awhile or do you want it often? If your partner's preferences are different than yours, it's going to feel demanding."

"So how do I negotiate the differences?" I ask.

My Fairy Godmom replies, "I don't think sex can be negotiated. It is to be recognized."

"What's the difference?" I ask.

"When you recognize, you don't need to negotiate with someone else. If you recognize that one of you wants sexual expression often and one of you doesn't, then there's the possibility for an acceptance that the rest of the relationship means a great deal and you begin to find the interplay of preferences. It's separation that provides the impetus for the climax. How much separate time do you have and how do you use it? How much separate time do you trust to one another? People are very afraid about who's going to be attracted to whom. Jealousy and competition consume a lot of energy. When you find people who are relaxed with themselves, you often find people who are relaxed with their sexuality also."

"I need to get away. Some days I feel like just walking out the door."

Many moms have two simple wishes: peace and quiet. We'd all like a little more than we currently have. I took my first soul vacation after 14 years as a mom. I had been on trips before but always *with* somebody—never by myself. At first, this was less of a soul vacation and more of a desperate act. This was a chance to have a hotel room all to myself. When my husband traveled for work, he would call each night from his hotel room. Our conversations followed an established format. I would begin by unloading about my day with the kids. He would tell me a little about his day. Then I would ask where he went for dinner and what the hotel was like. I was so envious that he'd had a good meal (that someone else prepared), a hotel room to himself, and a gym for his morning workout.

I outlined a few objectives for my trip: I wanted to be alone and spend my days and nights writing. I wanted to be able to exercise and eat well. Maybe I would drive up the California coast and rent a beach house. Maybe I would fly to a city that I'd never seen before. I didn't want to spend lots of time traveling, however. I knew I'd be just as happy staying at a hotel near my home.

I decided on a week at a local health resort, thirty minutes away. I had my own room and, best of all, someone was going to make my meals. The diet was a raw, vegan diet designed to detoxify the body. I understood the symptoms of physical detox, but I had no idea what emotional detox would be like. By Day Two, the detox was so intense that I drove home and tried to be needed. My husband didn't fall for it. He pointed out that he had taken a week's vacation to do this. He gave me an apple and sent me on my way.

For the first two days, he did well at home. On Day Three, a pleasant surprise occurred when I phoned home in the evening. My husband jabbered on and on about the kids, as though I was the only adult he had talked to all day. It was nice to discover that this tendency was situational rather than personal. And what about teaching my husband a lesson? It totally backfired. Not only did he enjoy the week with the kids, he also finished several home improvement projects. (That really got to me.) I discovered that there's more than my way to care for our children. Our styles are different, but the priorities are the same.

My Fairy Godmom reminds me that, "The more you insert yourself into the lives of your husband and children and the more you truly believe you are needed at home, the more needed you will be and the more you will want to get away. There's only a need to get away when one has created something that must be escaped. When you go away to write, you like knowing you have a home to go back to."

"I do," I say. "But I remember a time as a freelance writer when I didn't want to take vacations because I loved what I was doing."

"Right," she says. "There was nothing to get away from, and there isn't now. Wherever you go, you have you. So, what are you trying to get away from?" she asks.

"I'm trying to get away from how I am at home and how I react to my family. I'm not getting away from *who* I am as much as *how* I am," I say.

"Right again, so consider looking at how you use your time and space; how you are living out an ideal that isn't yours; how you're living out an image that's already gone. How do you make decisions? Even vacation time can be tightly scheduled with activities to help release built-up tensions. The media programming is 'to get away from it all,'" she replies.

"But sometimes I assume the same roles during our vacation that I do at home—like gatekeeper of meals or recreation director," I say.

"Yes," she says.

"Yes what?" I ask.

"Just yes," she smiles.

My second soul vacation was a visit to my brother and his wife. They're an early 30s couple with no children. They live on a 26-acre family farm, where it's several acres to the nearest neighbor and fifteen miles to town. I visited on the pretense of helping with harvest. My sister-in-law spends her free time in September and October putting up apples, pears, crab apples, and plums. On the 90-minute ride from the airport, I asked my brother about Houseguest 101—the basics on how our time together can be enjoyable for all. He summarized the course in one sentence: "Just get into your routine as quickly as possible."

On the first morning, I came out in my pajamas ready to cook breakfast for everybody. But nobody wanted breakfast. They were greeting the day. Doing yoga. Gathering things to take to the office. Making coffee. I unconsciously followed them around the house. If one of them walked into the kitchen, I did. When they got dressed, so did I. When they sat down with coffee at the kitchen table, I made myself a cup and sat down, too. I realized the absurdity of my behavior when I nearly followed my sister-in-law into the bathroom. I kept asking how I could help. They'd look around the house and shake their head. Nope, nothing really needed doing. I tried to be specific. Could I clean the kitchen while they were gone at work? Did the porch need sweeping? Should I start something for dinner? Could I do the laundry for them? In a moment of enlightenment, I finally said, "My behavior will make a lot more sense after you two have kids."

Mama Drama may be an avenue toward feeling important, useful, and helpful. But it's not the right kind of important, useful, and helpful because it's oriented outward. I shrunk my thinking to fit: I might do the dishes when my hands need to warm up—it's about 60 degrees in the house. I might cook dinner if I'm feeling inspired. I might sweep the porch if I want to take in some of the fall colors and crisp air. But the motivation will come from within.

"I don't know who I am anymore."

There was a time when I dreamed of having just a few minutes each day to myself. I found it. Then I dreamed of having two hours a day to myself. What an unheard-of luxury! I found that, too. Then I dreamed of having all three children in school at the same time, so that I could have mornings to myself. I shook with excitement as I imagined all I would accomplish. I might even finish my To Do List! I arranged for that time as well. Unbelievable. Who would have thought? Surely not me, and my lack of preparation is showing. What's missing is my ability to precisely define what "time to myself" means. I have the time, but I don't have the self—just yet.

I'm busy. Isn't everyone? I'm doing the productive things that go along with managing a family of five: bill paying, grocery shopping, cooking, cleaning, and carpooling. I have two freelance projects and a book manuscript in the works, but I'm spending the least amount of time on the activities that matter the most to me.

Maybe I ought to clarify my definition of "productive." I start with *Webster's II New Riverside Dictionary*. It says,

pro·duce

1. To bring forth by a natural process: yield.

2. To bring about: create. 3. To make by a special

process: manufacture. 4. To cause to exist: give rise to.

Hmmm . . . where's the part about filling time with tasks that I think I should care about? Perhaps I should write *Webster's III, New Mom's Dictionary*.

Nothing I'm doing has the quality of a "natural process." I'm not "bringing about or making anything by a special process," unless forcing qualifies as special. I'm not even "causing to exist or giving rise to." I mistakenly believe that what I'm doing is productive—because it's filling time— and I shudder to think of myself as anything less than productive with my time. But I don't see time anywhere in this definition.

What if I took one moment to be aware of what "productive" means to me? Let's see what happens. I start by listing hundreds of things that I want to do with my time. No need to elaborate, you know The List. What I'm still overlooking though is the quality of the moments. It's not necessarily what I do but rather how I feel when I'm doing it. I write because of how I feel when I'm writing. I spend time with my family because of the joy it brings me. I fix up the house because when I look at what I've done, it makes me happy. I exercise because of how I feel when I exercise. (Okay, I usually feel best after I exercise, but you get the idea.)

The richest moments, I'm discovering, are those in which time disappears and I'm aware of my connection to both sides of life—the seen and the unseen. It's when I'm aware of having one focus with many paths heading toward it. I can take any path, but quality of self is paramount. I am a work-in-progress. I am Webster's incarnate: being brought forth by a natural process; yielding; bringing about and creating; causing to exist and giving rise to. I'm so productive, there's no definition for it!

My Fairy Godmom asks, "How often do we consider that our attitudes affect our actions? Our actions affect the situation. We give life to and personalize the events through our attitudes."

What does motherhood feel like to you? Go back to the moment that you decided to become a mom.

- Were you escaping from the business world into motherhood? If so, motherhood may feel like a dreaded job.

- Did you have a child to fulfill an image you had of being a mom? If so, you may feel ignored as a mom or you may demand your child's attention.

- Were you avoiding having to do something else? If so, you may feel like it's difficult to be responsible for a child.

- Was it unexpected? If so, you may feel like you have no control over your experience as a mom.

Any significant change begins with a process of identifying where we are. We know where we are when we know where we've been. Choices start when we identify what we **don't** want. From there, it's imperative that we take action and move toward what we **do** want. My Fairy Godmom says, "Look at your track record. It's your fortune teller and predicts where you are going, unless you choose to change your habitual reactions."

What you may discover is that you *decided* to become a mom for one reason and *continue* to be a mom for many others.

"During summer, I feel like the Head Counselor at Camp Mom."

I used to dread summertime. Somewhere along my image-gathering journey, I picked up the idea that part of my job was to be the Head Counselor at Camp Mom. A great summer for me means that the TV, computer, and video games stay off all day and as much of the night as possible. For the children, a great summer means exactly the opposite.

Our Official Summer Litany usually opens with, "Mom, I'm bored."

I respond with, "How can you be bored? You have so many toys. What do you want to do? Do you want to play a game, call a friend, go somewhere, do a craft, make cookies?" I used to believe that entertaining the children was part of being a Good Mom. It felt like a have-to, though, not a want-to. Big difference.

The first summer that I retired from my job as Head Counselor was also the first summer that I truly enjoyed. It happened when my children were 15, 7, and 3. Rather than working to keep them busy, I started planning summer around a wish of mine: I wanted the first two weeks of summer mornings to myself in order to make headway on this manuscript. My oldest was scheduled for a two-week vacation with his grandparents, so I looked for two weeks of half-day camps for my younger boys. As summer approached, my plan was almost in place, except that my 7-year-old had only one week of camp instead of two. Try as I did to locate an appealing camp with an opening, it wasn't falling into place, but something else was. My husband had been downsized out of a job at the end of April. I assumed that by summertime, he would have another job, but he didn't. Perhaps he could take care of our 7-year-old for a week.

My old approach to getting what I wanted usually involved dramatic body language: sighing, frowning, and sending the occasional blast of stink eye until my husband finally asked, "Are you okay?" This time, I took a more mature approach. I calmly explained my wish for two weeks of mornings to myself. Then I asked him (in a very nonjudgmental way—which I have been trained to do) if he would be willing to take our son and be out of the house every morning for a week. He said "yes" and asked for some ideas on what the two of them could do. In the end, I got the time that I wanted, and my husband even took the boys to and from camp so that the house was quiet a little longer.

I was fortified by this outcome, so I set about pursuing my next wish: to read some children's classics. I dug out my stash of reading lists (part of my Good Mom program) and read it to my two younger boys. "Okay you guys, what do you want to read from this list?" I asked cheerfully.

My 7-year-old stared at me and said plainly, "Nothing, Mom. *You* want to read from that list." Out of the mouths of babes, huh? I went to the library and checked out *Charlotte's Web*. The first night, as I read it aloud on the couch just before bedtime, no one joined me. However, on the second night, they snuggled in close. It wasn't a have-to; it was a want-to. Big difference.

A few nights later, I needed to clear my head after a disagreement with my husband, so I set up the tent in our backyard and slept outside. The next night, the boys decided that they wanted to read *Charlotte's Web* in the tent with flashlights. They ended up sleeping outside for a week.

The more I begin with myself, the more I find my children joining me. I remember my favorite "mom-tra": Being myself is more important than being mom; being myself will take care of being mom.

"Even though I'm somebody's mom, there's so much I don't know."

One mom says, "You're only as old as your oldest child. You progress as a mom up to the oldest child, but beyond that you don't know yet."

When my oldest was five, I could recognize and relate to children who were five or younger, but I had no idea about older children. The parents of teenagers would look lovingly at my 5-year-old and say, "Enjoy it while you can. They grow up fast." I felt like I was enjoying it—as much as I could at the 5-year-old stage. Yet, there was still so much I didn't know. I wondered how I would ever learn what I needed to know for what was down the road.

My Fairy Godmom reminds me that, "The solution to many situations as a mom is to say, 'I don't know.' Admit what you don't know. Saying, 'I don't care' is totally different. The intent behind saying 'I don't know' is 'let's find out together.' Otherwise, there's this conviction that at some point in your life, you're going to know everything— like your mom and dad did, right?"

It was then that I realized there's no reason for me to read up on teenagers, because I was several years away. And, as many of us learned in pregnancy, there's only so much preparation one can do. At some point, we must step into the experience for our next stage of growth. What can we do now to learn about our future? Participate in the experiences that are in front of us.

"I want us to spend more time as a family."

I have images of my family trekking Europe, visiting national parks, and beach camping in Baja—images directly out of the Patagonia Catalog, I might add. My images include all of us having a terrific time together, learning about new places, and coming home with rich memories. (By the way, there's nothing in my images about illness, itinerary changes, park closures, inclement weather, or travel costs.)

So why aren't we traveling?

Most likely because of a small point that I overlooked: reality. My husband left his job to start his own company at the same time that our teenager took a job to save for a car. As I was telling a friend about my wish for more family travel, I realized that the family time I wanted was happening—at home. For me, time away equaled family memories, and time away equaled time together. Applying the transitive property of addition here means that time together equals family memories—wherever we are.

I have to look beyond my image to this: I want my children to travel. Is it okay for them to travel without me? One summer, my family took separate vacations. My husband took our two younger boys to visit relatives. Our oldest son traveled with his grandfather, and I went camping with some friends. A week later, we all returned and swapped stories. Our oldest son went body boarding in Hawaii for the first time. My husband and our two younger boys spent time with cousins, aunts, uncles, and grandparents. I camped with three friends on a deserted beach, went snorkeling, and took naps in the afternoon.

My Fairy Godmom says that, "When everybody goes off in different directions and comes back, you have the whole world to share. If you go be you and I go be me, when we come together we have this big world to share. To do that with children is wonderful. It's Life."

"I worry that my kids spend too much time in front of the TV and the computer."

My Fairy Godmom reminds me that, "Whatever you focus on gives it life." This is a law of physics. Therefore, if I'm determined to **not** have my children watch television, I'm actually focusing on what I **don't** want them to do. That gives it life. I've read articles on TV-free households, and I agree with the benefits. However, when I undertook my own "Nintendo® Experiment," here's what I discovered: By being so outspoken against having Nintendo® in my home, I was drawing my children's attention to Nintendo®. My oldest son kept asking if he could bring Grandma's Nintendo® over to our house. He wouldn't let up. Finally, I gave in and let him bring Nintendo® home for a weekend. My children were hooked. They didn't eat. They didn't respond to simple instructions. I had focused so much on **not** having Nintendo® around that it was all they wanted.

Over the years, I've relaxed my rules about TV viewing. We still don't have Nintendo® and I don't like TV any more than I used to, but I'm more pro-active about it now. Rather than spending my time huffing around or handing out poker chips so the boys can buy TV time, I focus on other things. If the boys ask to watch TV, I ask whether their chores and homework are taken care of. If so, they have free time to spend. In this relaxed atmosphere, TV doesn't have the draw that it used to.

Today, my 5-year-old came home from preschool with a runny nose and looking like he needed a rest. I said he could watch TV while he rested on the couch. I went upstairs to take a shower. When I came downstairs to check on him, it was unusually quiet. As I peered into the family room, I saw that the TV was off and that he had fallen asleep on the couch. I couldn't have asked for a more perfect result, but it didn't come from forcing him to take a nap. Instead, it came from setting an atmosphere of relaxation. I had put pillows and a blanket around him and rubbed essential oils on his chest and feet. I had turned off the telephone and left the room. He took it from there. Whatever we focus on gives it life.

"The world feels so unsafe right now."

My Fairy Godmom reminds me that, "This stuff has been around forever. Only now, the news runs on a continuous loop. It's this repetition that often makes us feel unsafe. Where are you putting your attention? What's the source of your fear? Are you fearful about your current situation or are you bringing a fear from childhood, from a news report, or even from talking with friends and family? Sometimes we make a drama by inserting ourselves into another's experience, and we use the drama as if it's our own. Consider shifting your attention to what your child reminds you of every day about life. No commercial interruptions allowed."

"How can I get my kids to eat well?"

It's Halloween—a sugar-coated holiday that I dread. I attended my kindergartener's class party and almost keeled over when I saw what was offered:

- Cheetos®

- Cracker Jacks®

- Chocolate cupcakes with green frosting and a cookie tombstone

- White cupcakes with orange and black frosting

- Glazed donuts with colored sprinkles

I resolved then and there to find something healthier for this year's trick-or-treaters. Imagine my delight when I came across a large bag of 40 individually wrapped pretzel packages—the kind the airlines hand out. I proudly announced to my children that we would be handing out something healthy for Halloween instead of candy.

"What?!" my 13-year-old exploded. "Pretzels? Mom, no one likes pretzels for Halloween. That's so lame. No one's even going to come to our house!" I was ready for this reaction from a teenager. However, when my 24-year-old babysitter suggested that handing out pennies might be more exciting than pretzels, I re-evaluated my approach.

Despite educating myself on healthy eating, I rarely get my children to eat what I know is healthy for them. My continuing interest in healthy eating is sometimes more of a curse than a blessing, as I raise the bar on what constitutes healthy fare. After 20 years of cooking for a family, mealtime was becoming tense and full of negotiations. I was frustrated while cooking because I knew that at least one person in my family wouldn't like what was served.

Around this time, I attended a lecture given by women's advocate, Gregge Tiffen. He advises women to avoid cooking when they're angry. "Never, never, never, cook if you're angry," he says. "You're killing your family. Never do that. I mean it's better to go to McDonald's—twice a week if you have to. Don't cook when you're angry. What you put into that food turns out to be pure poison. Now, it isn't going to show up that night, but it's going to show up . . . If you're really mad, just don't go into the kitchen." (When eating out, the same principle applies. Leave the restaurant if you sense there's tension in the kitchen.)

His advice stayed with me. Later, I learned that a Kirlian photograph (Kirlian shows the energy around an object) showed food before and after it had been blessed. The aura around the blessed food glowed with vitality. When I added that information to the value I placed on organic farming, a new approach to feeding my family started to swirl. It wasn't just what I cooked but where the food came from and my attitude in preparing it. I knew things had to change in my home, because if I was cooking healthy food in frustration, I was doing more harm than good.

I addressed my lack of inspiration by offering each child a night to choose a meal and prepare it together. For weeks, we ate macaroni and cheese on Mondays, pizza on Tuesdays, and tacos on Wednesdays. It wasn't too long before the boys understood the meaning of burnout. From there, we looked for inspiration. We asked grandmothers for family recipes. We morphed fast food favorites into healthier choices at home. We borrowed ideas from neighbors. We found pizza crusts at the healthy food store, so we had build-your-own pizza night. We re-created the breakfast burritos from our favorite local restaurant. It was much more fun to prepare meals with my family rather than for them. Slowly, I released my white-knuckled grip around the ideal diet and opted for peace of mind.

My Fairy Godmom reminds me that, "Anytime you think there is a way something should be done, you're working with a fantasy. Do the current conditions support your fantasy? If so, it's reality." She suggested that I take the emphasis off of food and focus on cooking up the atmosphere that I wanted for my family at dinnertime. "What type of gathering reflects what matters most to you?" she asked.

I went home and found my grandmother's silverware from 1929. I had inherited it, and for the ten years since her death, it had been sitting in a box at the top of the linen closet. Next, I bought pure beeswax candles and lit one each night before dinner. Eating by the light of a single candle was too dark, so I dimly lit the chandelier above the table and turned off all the lights in the rest of the house. The focus was on an inviting dinner table. I also decided to serve the food family style—no more deciding who should eat how much of what. I established one rule for mealtime: "You don't have to eat, but you do have to meet." In other words, mealtime is about gathering more than eating.

I love dinner again. I said to my Fairy Godmom, "You know, the kids seem just as healthy, even though we may not be eating as well as we used to."

She replied, "Healthier, actually, because they have the memories of the companionship to digest."

"I lose track of myself."

My Fairy Godmom says, "To the degree that you ignore your own life, you will insert yourself into the lives of others."

Says Anna, a newly single mom to 9-year-old Jordan, "I had an epiphany last week. I realized that the further I stay out of Kyle's [her ex-husband's] orbit, the better. It's taken an incredible amount of emotional and physical energy playing 'clean up' and trying to insure that Jordan feels loved and has a firm sense of stability. Jordan told me yesterday, unprompted, that she would like to live with me full-time. That may be the right thing, though it makes me sad for her. We'll just have to see. As for me, I am enjoying my new life when I'm not being reactive to Jordan and Kyle's situation."

Anna senses clearly when the switch to Mama Drama occurs for her and when she loses her wisdom. She's trying to negotiate the changing dynamic between her ex-husband and their only child. Although Kyle cares for his daughter, he's not caring in the way that Anna cares for her. Anna realizes that she loses herself and her power when she interferes in their relationship.

We can learn to be less involved with others. We can stay close to those activities that give us pleasure and watch our self-identity take root again. One thing we can do for ourselves that nobody else can do for us is to breathe. Then, breathe again.

"I often act out of selfishness."

Family and friends used to accuse me of worrying and being overprotective. Looking deeper, I realized that my motivation was selfishness. Here's one scenario:

My 5-year-old is jumping into the pool from the edge. He's doing that sideways jump that children do when they're learning to swim—the one that puts the wall within arm's reach. I say, "Jackson, you need to jump further away from the edge."

My dad is there and he says, "Julie, he's fine. Why do you have to worry so much?" My blood pressure starts its ascent.

"Dad," I say, "If he jumps too close to the edge and bangs his head on the side or knocks out a few teeth or whams his chin and needs stitches, who do you think he's going to go to? Me. I'm the one who will comfort him, drive him to the emergency room, wait at least two hours to see a doctor, deal with his pain, and deal with the bills. I don't want to do that."

This all sounds very logical as I say it, but upon reflection, I realize that I'm playing out my Mama Drama. I have choices. I can leave the pool area and put someone else in charge of watching him. I can ask someone else to take him to the emergency room, too. My husband can take him. Heck, my dad can take him. My son is a beloved child—of this, I am sure.

I remember a time when I wanted to exercise first thing in the morning. My husband thought this was a terrific idea, and he agreed to cook breakfast and take the boys to school. This was a great arrangement—for about two weeks. That's when I started criticizing what my husband was packing for school lunches and pointing out that the boys didn't have clean clothes on. What I really missed was seeing my boys in the morning before school. I returned to my routine with more clarity about how and when I want to participate in my children's lives. Choices are everywhere.

(Hey, no words from my Fairy Godmom on this issue. I must be catching on!)

"Before I had children, I used to say, 'No child of mine would be allowed to _____.'"

How do we know what our mothering style will be if we've never had the experience? Remember all the great ideas you had about children before you became a parent? We believe that we can choose the kind of mom we will be ahead of time: Stay-at-home mom. Cookies-and-milk mom. Working mom. Single mom. Married mom. Yet we don't choose the kind of children we will be mothers to. Do you know a woman who is pregnant with her first child who has already figured out how motherhood will fit into her life? Perhaps she's arranged for daycare because she's returning to work after the baby arrives. Maybe she's signed up her baby at the best preschool because she's sure it's the one she wants him/her to attend.

How often do these plans really work out the way we expect them to? We had control over our bodies prior to conception. Then, we spiraled out of control as our body and mind experienced pregnancy, labor, and delivery. Those of us who planned to return to work may have overlooked the dance that develops between mother and baby. Those of us who intended to devote our lives to giving our children the best of everything may have neglected our need for a life apart from our children—a life where we can learn new steps for our dance. Even if we decide how our lives will look after we become mothers, we're only guessing. What we do know is that we signed up for the experience of motherhood. As we face each experience, we instinctively know what we want from that experience.

My Fairy Godmom says, "When we take each experience as it comes, we grow beyond what we ever imagined. If we have preconceptions, there's no room for new discoveries to occur."

"I want to be fair to all my kids."

"Fair" is a four-letter word. As children, we're taught to do what's fair for everybody. Then suddenly, somewhere in young adulthood, we find out that life isn't fair. Yipes! One of the best things we can do for our children is to recognize their differences. That's the fair thing to do. Each of them has different needs for attention, education, sleep, time with mom and dad, time with friends, food, privileges, travel, after-school activities, etc.

Fairness runs rampant around birthdays and holidays when we insist on measuring gifts by quantity or cost. We're operating so far from the essence of giving that it's shameful. Remember what it feels like to give out of inspiration? I have a friend who gives only from inspiration. As he moved away from obligatory giving and toward inspired giving, he was a hot topic on the family grapevine. But I never forgot the feeling when a true gift arrived. Months away from my birthday or a holiday, a book that he wanted me to have or a photo that reminded him of good times would arrive on my doorstep.

Some on the grapevine said that young children shouldn't have to deal with this type of gift-giving because it sets them up for disappointment. What exactly sets them up for disappointment? The person who gives from inspiration, or the person who draws the child's attention to birthdays and holidays with images of all the goodies they'll receive? This is a terrific first step for putting a stop to Mama Drama. Are you giving from a place of desire or a place of duty . . . from inspiration or obligation? And you say you're too tired for sex? Hmmm.

My Fairy Godmom says, "Once you start living with some imagination, you'll find that inspiration and desire gain momentum."

"Sometimes I feel like it's me against the world."

When I feel overwhelmed, my Fairy Godmom reminds me to go back to my original intent. One Sunday while playing with friends, my 7-year-old tripped and fell on the driveway. He had a half-inch gash on his eyebrow that needed stitches. Because this would be his first emergency room visit, I opted for the children's hospital ER rather than Urgent Care. As expected, the doctors were very accommodating and thorough. However, because it was a Sunday afternoon, getting him four stitches took 4 hours! Actual prep and stitching time was about 90 minutes.

Three weeks later, my insurance company sent an Explanation of Benefits. I had been charged $500 for "surgery and materials" and another $1,130 for "health services." Over $1,600 for four stitches. The situation was ripe for Mama Drama. I could have babbled my injustice to everyone I talked to that day. I could have postured to get others to ask what was bothering me. I could have done many things to continue the drama, but I decided not to. I realized that if I went back to my original intent—a clear decision to take my son to the children's hospital—that the same energy would carry me through this. Money wasn't a consideration in my original decision, and I wasn't about to make it one because of a piece of paper that, at the moment, required no action on my part. I reviewed my past experiences with insurance companies:

- Was somebody asking for payment right now? No.
- In my experience, had an insurance company ever made a processing error? All the time.

– In my experience, had medical bills ever been inaccurate?

Absolutely.

For now, the best I could do was to use the wisdom from my past experiences. That meant waiting until I received a bill to take further action. When the bill arrived two months later, I found that my insurance company had negotiated a lower fee and I was able to finance the remainder, interest-free.

"I want to spend more time with my children."

My Fairy Godmom asks, "What kind of time? When? What time of day do you want to be with them? What time of day is the very most fun for you to be with your children? Does this time of day change according to their ages? Does this time of day change according to your age? This is about knowing that we all have choices. Do your children want to be with you all the time? Look again. Be honest. It's humbling, isn't it?

"If you want to have more time with your children, is that because you think that when they get older, you're going to regret that you didn't? My nephew Todd says, 'Regrets are great because they let you live more than one life at a time.' Ask yourself if what you want is really more time with your children or is it that you hear people saying, 'Kids grow up so fast'? Time is an outside factor that is put upon us. It interferes with and disrupts rhythm and harmony. Father Time can be a benevolent father or a stern taskmaster. Mother Nature operates in cycles. How are you thinking about time?"

I'm thinking that it's 4:30 p.m., and I have no idea what's for dinner. I need to go grocery shopping, but I can't leave now. There are five boys hanging out in my driveway. They're not doing anything special. They're just children enjoying a summer day.

A few weeks ago, the same thing happened to my husband. I asked him to call the children in to get ready for bed. He went out the front door and returned too soon. "What happened?" I asked.

He shook his head. "I can't call 'em in Julie. They're having too much fun," he smiled. They had a neighborhood game of roller hockey going. Sometimes, it's skate boarders and in-line skaters doing tricks on the collection of ramps, rails, and boxes that they've built. The activity doesn't matter as much as the flow. It's child time, and it can't be interrupted.

How do I know it can't be interrupted? Because I've tried many times, and here's what usually happens. When I tell the children it's time to clean up so we can go grocery shopping for dinner, the whining starts. Then there's the lost shoe or the neighbor kid who can't remember where he put his bike helmet. While they clean up under protest, I write out a grocery list. That's when the telephone rings. Without thinking, I answer it. It's a long-distance call from an old friend. She has news. The children stand around. They start bickering. They glare at me. Finally, I hang up. We get to the store, and another argument begins over who will sit in the cart and who will push the cart. The check-out lines are usually longer around dinner time. We arrive home, and I start cooking. That's when I remember the one main ingredient that I forgot to buy. We have to call out for pizza.

This time, I know better. I know I'm happier enjoying a warm summer afternoon with my children rather than dragging them through an air-conditioned supermarket. I'll figure out something for dinner—even if it's breakfast for dinner. Then it happens—a moment of synchronicity. I notice one of my neighbors (who works in the food industry) walking towards me carrying a large plastic bag. "You guys like pasta?" he asks.

"Yes, we do!" I smile.

"Would you like these? They're leftover samples from what I had from today." He hands me the bag. I knew I had marinara sauce in the freezer and plenty of zucchini in the garden.

"Marc, thanks," I say. "You just brought us dinner."

I wanted to spend this time with my children more than I wanted to make dinner. I took care of myself, and dinner took care of itself.

"I feel so responsible for my children's health. I want to give them a good start."

My Fairy Godmom asks, "What do you know about health that supports your children? What does your track record indicate to you?"

Here's my track record: When my first child was ill, I dutifully took him to the pediatrician. This is what Good Moms do, right? The waiting room was divided; sick kids on one side of the room, well kids on the other—the ol' smoking/non-smoking logic. The receptionist darted around like a humming bird checking in patients, answering phones, and checking out patients. We were escorted back to an exam room, where we waited 10 minutes for the doctor. After a 7-minute consultation, we left with a prescription for an antibiotic. A few months later, we would be at the doctor's office with the same illness.

When my second child came down with two ear infections before he was 4 months old, I knew what conventional medicine had to offer. Knowing this, I sought out a homeopath. The idea of strengthening the immune system made sense to me, so I wanted to learn more. My experience was immediately different. When I called for an appointment, the receptionist was relaxed and didn't put me on hold three times. The doctor was able to see us that same day. The waiting room was soothing. Soft music played. There were plants, a few toys, and a bottled-water dispenser. The homeopath talked with our family for an hour. She wanted to know about diet, sleep patterns, and behaviors. By following her advice and educating myself on alternative treatments, none of my children ever had ear infections again.

Still, when they would catch a cold or the flu, it was tempting to ignore my previous experience and take them to the pediatrician. However, the same thing happened. We'd leave with a prescription and deal with the same virus a few months later. Finally, I learned—but not before one last visit to the pediatrician's office. This time, I walked into the waiting room, heard crying coming from kids in the exam rooms, saw runny-nosed toddlers playing with toys, and tired parents gazing at the walls. I asked the receptionist if the doctor was running on time. She was 20 minutes behind, so I cancelled the appointment and never returned. I took my son to a chiropractor, and she treated him. In three days, he was well.

My Fairy Godmom reminds me of the differences between images and values. "Images lack meaning and depth. Values are images that have been field-tested." She asks me, "How do you recognize your values?"

When my 4-year-old was sick recently, I tried a new approach by asking him what he thought would make him better. He knows about "sugar pills" (homeopathic pellets), "oils" (therapeutic-grade essential oils), and "herbs" (Chinese herbs from our practitioner). He also knows Dr. Mein (our chiropractor) and Nobu Asano (our Traditional Chinese Medicine Practitioner). Talking with him means that he and I are allies. I can help him make decisions about his health by walking through his choices with him, instead of telling him how he's going to get well. The truth is, I have no idea what combination will make him well. But at 4, he's blessed with an unspoiled intuition. And guess what? It worked.

Now, I'm less dramatic about the children' health. They still get sick, but not as seriously as they used to. We've been antibiotic-free for five years now. As my Fairy

Godmom says, "Angels can fly because they take themselves lightly."

"I just don't feel ready to have a child."

Says women's advocate Gregge Tiffen, "A woman's body is designed for childbearing, but that's not an obligation; it's an option."

Jan, a mother of one, says, "Maybe it's time we, as a society, supported women if their real choice would be not to have kids at all—instead of calling them 'selfish' or 'incomplete women.' Let's face it, some women are not cut out to be moms, and we need to support them more fully so they don't go ahead and have a child or two because that's what they're supposed to do. I have three very good friends who are not mothers by their choice. Hardly selfish women, they contribute substantially to our community and lead very interesting lives . . . actually they're some of the most nurturing women I know."

I have an amazing cousin. She's 43 and child-free. One year for my birthday she sent me a plane ticket to visit her for the weekend. She offered me a guest room, adult conversation, time to enjoy a shower and get dressed for dinner, and a look at how life is without children. We spent time talking, hiking, seeing a movie, eating together, enjoying coffee, and visiting open houses in a neighborhood that she'd like to move into. I came home refreshed from the rest, inspired by what's down the road for me when my children are grown, and grateful for her time and energy in sharing her lifestyle.

Closing the Curtain on Mama Drama

Much of the energy we are putting into motherhood revolves around gaining respect in our role as mothers. How are we going to recognize respect, appreciation, and compassion from others if we don't first offer these to ourselves? What would these values look like in our lives? How would they feel? Where would they come from?

My Fairy Godmom reminds me that, "Every single woman has something to offer. Mothers are the saints of the culture because they really, really are doing something unnoticed and extremely important. It is up to each one of us to appreciate ourselves."

CHAPTER 3

To The Dads

MY FAIRY GODMOM SAYS, "TOWARD THE END OF THE PREGNANCY, DADS-TO-BE REALIZE THAT WHAT WAS ONCE JUST A CONCEPT [HMM, CONCEPTION] IS NOW TURNING INTO A CONVICTION.

Something is about to happen 'unto them' that surpasses anything that can be accurately understood, let alone explained. As much as they want the baby and truly love their wife, what to do? How to do it? And most of all, how long is this phase going to last? I MISS MY WIFE!

"Toward the end of the pregnancy, some women need to

settle into their surroundings and gather strength from their peace of mind. If you, as dads, insist on discussing future plans such as moving, taking a new job, or anything that has a hint of disrupting a secure and stable environment, watch out! Timing is everything, and there will be plenty of time after the baby is born to make plans again. Let such thoughts gestate within you."

Your wife needs to rest and decompress more often than even she wants to admit. She needs to talk and know that you're listening. It's essential that she is able to share her feelings of doubt, her fears, and her excitement about pregnancy and motherhood with you, the most intimate person in her life.

Key point: Your wife does not need solutions. This is not personal to you. That's worth repeating to yourself often— **This is not personal.** She simply wants to hear how she thinks, and you are a wonderful sounding board. If she wants help, she'll ask for your advice. If you're tempted to offer solutions, first ask her if she wants advice or an idea on solving her problem. If she's not interested in what you have to offer, she probably just needs to decompress. Let her. After all, you may be the only caring adult she's talked to all day.

After Baby: Working Dads and Stay-at-Home Moms

One expert has said that a woman who stays home with

children needs one full day a week to herself. Let's face it, some women consider themselves lucky if they can shower alone. If you're a working dad, and your wife stays home with the children, this section is worth your attention for peace of mind.

In short, we stay-at-home moms can benefit from some time away. My husband (Brian) and I agree on this, but we've had a rocky start. Somehow, he believes that if I'm at home, I must be watching the children. It's my job when he's not around, so why mess up a good thing, right? My brother-in-law does the same thing with my sister. She's figured out that it's smarter for her to leave the house if she wants time to herself rather than stick around and risk confusing her husband (and the children) as to who's in charge.

Here's what happened today. Brian came home for lunch, saying that he had two hours before he had to be back at the office. He offered to watch our 3-year-old so I could "take some time for myself." This is the politically correct phrase that he uses in place of former phrases like, "Hey Honey, I'll watch the kids so you can go to the gym." This phrase elicited all sorts of reactive questions from me like, "Are you saying that I need to go to the gym? You think I'm fat, don't you? Do these pants make my butt look big?" In Brian's mind, watching the children used to mean that I now had time to do something productive, like working out, changing the oil in the mini-van, or repainting the house.

I accepted Brian's offer and explained to him in a calm, non-threatening way (as I have been trained to do) that Carsen needed a nap because he was fighting a cold virus. "No problem," said Brian. So I ducked into my writing studio. Fifteen minutes later, Brian walked in and said, "Okay, Carsen's asleep now."

"Great, thanks," I said and gave him the you-can-leave-now look. I returned to what I was doing, half wondering why he interrupted me to say that Carsen was sleeping. I don't call him at the office to tell him that the children are playing outside. Oh well, back to what I was doing.

I needed Brian's signature on a form, so I walked downstairs. "Brian? Brian?" I whispered. It was too quiet. I walked out the front door and noticed that his car was gone. Apparently, the "time to myself" had ended 30 minutes ago, but I didn't realize it.

Sound familiar? It happened often enough that I drafted something called, *Guidelines for My Time*. Your wife could have written these just as easily as I did. She and I hope you'll take a minute to read through this.

Guidelines for My Time

Loosely translated, "My Time" means the time during which

I am not expected to watch the kids or be responsible for them in any way, except legally. Although it may look, to you, like I have plenty of free time when the kids are napping, the truth is, I'm still responsible for them. It would help immensely if you could remind me to schedule My Time on a regular basis by letting me know exactly when you will be caring for our kids. That way, I have no other choice but to take My Time.

First, My Time is not your time. This means that it is not up to you how I spend My Time. If I want to call a girlfriend and have an uninterrupted phone conversation, terrific. If I decide to go grocery shopping in peace, fine. However, if all I'm capable of is sitting and watching you dance around the demands of our children, then I'm entitled to do that as well. And if I do that, my promise to you is that I will have only compassion (and not criticism) for you.

Second, I am unavailable during My Time—except for true emergencies (life and limb kinda stuff). That means that even if I'm within reach, you will handle all issues related to pooping, throwing up, breaking of household items, policing TV time, refereeing sibling rivalry, and responding to requests for food, toys, friends to play with, more food, different games, rides to friends' houses, and more food.

Third, if I return from My Time before you've been able to clean up what has occurred during your time with the kids,

I'll be happy to care for the kids while you clean up the mess.

My Promise to You: While I'm away, I understand that our kids and the household tasks will be cared for in YOUR WAY and at YOUR PACE. I will avoid commenting on how things should be done in my absence or what wasn't done at all. Instead, I will indicate in some way my gratitude for all you did to give me time away. I promise to return home renewed and happy. (Suggest that wife initial this last sentence.)

About Sex

Foreplay starts at breakfast.

CHAPTER 4

From Mama Drama to Dalai Mama

NE DAY, I REALIZED I HAD CHANGED.

It was in the evening when a new awareness crept up behind me, tapped my shoulder, and smiled. Here I was, giving my 4-year-old a bath. Only I wasn't giving anything at the moment. For once, I wasn't telling him what to do after his bath or negotiating when we would wash his hair. For once, I was still, quiet, and detached. The tears welled up in my eyes, and I realized that I was feeling again! Once turned into twice and twice turned into three times. From there, I lost count. It was becoming a habit. A habit of being—not just doing.

The difference is not so much in *what* we do but *how* we do it. Let's see how our Queen of Mama Drama has transformed into a Dalai Mama. We'll use the pronoun "I" this time:

- Rather than inserting myself into disagreements to which I am not a party, I allow children, family members, and friends to work out their differences. If I want to be supportive, I can offer non-verbal assistance—like time and space for people to meet in an atmosphere of acceptance and safety.

- Rather than orchestrating my children's social calendars, I understand that at a certain age children are capable of dialing a phone, asking for their friend, and making plans. When they need to figure out timing or transportation, they'll consult an adult.

- I combine tradition with imagination.

- I know better than to offer unsolicited advice. I remind myself that I have learned more from experience.

- I say, "no" when I need to say "no" and "yes" when I need to say "yes."

- I allow my children to discover their own interests and abilities in school, sports, club projects, and social life.
- I know that each moment begins with "m-o-m."
- I understand boredom because even I get bored sometimes! I offer my children and myself pure, uninterrupted time and space.
- I spend time on activities that enrich me.
- I am mindful of my values.
- I trust that silence is loving communication.
- I ask for help when I need it, and I appreciate what I learn if my helper accomplishes the task in a different way than I expect.
- I appreciate that everyone has an emotional value system that is forever evolving, just as mine is.
- I take time for myself naturally, without forcing the issue.
- I do things for myself with my children.

The idea is to progress from mystified (and therefore dramatic) to mystical (authentic) by building on what you know about the best in yourself. The mystified mom believes that her children are preventing her from being who she really wants to be and truly is. Consider that it may not be the children, but rather who she wants to be in their lives. If she wants to be all-mom 24/7, then where are the other parts of her?

A Dalai Mama invites her children on a journey of authenticity. For her, quality of self is paramount. She understands natural progression and embraces experience. My Fairy Godmom reminds me that, "Your beliefs come from what you have experienced. Your power is already there, but the belief factor may not be in place. Often, people don't believe in themselves and then they blame outside conditions or other people. The reason? They are abdicating their individual power and, therefore, individual responsibility. The solution? Identify just one thing that thrills you about you and be aware of using that power. There is energy in power. This power comes from an inner conviction that is very old and very wise. It's you. To find it, begin using it."

A Dalai Mama is willing to shift her awareness and attention as necessary to keep her elegant spirit within. She is aware of the layers (people, processes, images, and more) in life that can keep authenticity at a distance. She realizes that mothers are every child's connection to inner wisdom. Mothers are connected to each of us physically from the moment we take form and spiritually forever after.

Finding A Fairy Godmom

Says my Fairy Godmom, "I woke up early this morning with this phrase on my mind: chain of command. It related to older women sharing with younger ones. I thought of my mother, who I had less and less in common with as I grew up, but I still treasure many things about her and our relationship. The one I miss the most is that whenever I wanted to share something funny, I would call her and it became even funnier. We often shared delicious laughter. The women friends I have who are older than I am offer a perspective with a kind of caring and humor that seems to come from experience combined with acceptance. They have taught me the difference between resignation and acceptance."

Is there a woman whose spirit, philosophy, and experience inspire you? Her comments awaken in you what you already know but had put to sleep. It's as if something familiar and yet something new is being communicated when you are with her. To check in with her on a regular basis becomes easier during a phone call, a tea party, or a walk. We can learn to listen to our own wise woman in the presence of an older woman who chooses honest communication. Sometimes, it is just her silent presence, and other times she is willing to speak up if we become hardened in our attitudes and hard of hearing.

What a Fairy Godmom is *not*:

- She's not involved in your personal affairs.

- She's not invasive.

- She doesn't call to find out how you're doing.

- She's not your coach because she is not involved in getting results.

What a Fairy Godmom *is*:

- She's someone who is as interested in you as you are meant to be in yourself.

- She's aware of the value of experience.

- She trusts awareness to be an ongoing adventure, not to be hurried.

- She has a wonder-filled life of her own.

- She treasures the mystery of being a woman.

Remember these adages, "When the student is ready, the teacher will appear. When the question is honest, the answer is revealed." If you truly want a Fairy Godmom, you will find each other. If you'd like, we can share my Fairy Godmom. (See *Contact Us* at the back of the book.)

Your Fairy Godmom may be one woman, or there may be

several Fairy Godmoms in your queendom. Once we accept that such real support is possible, we begin an adventure that none of us wants to miss: the finding and the allowing, the sharing and the support that enriches our lives as women, lovers, wives, and mothers as we learn what it means to be a woman first.

- ACKNOWLEDGMENTS -

From Julie . . .

The following people have contributed, each in a different way, to bringing this book from heart to hands. I am deeply grateful to Patrece, Gregge, Brian, Jake, Jackson, Carsen, Woods, Holly, Della, Jan, Monie, Steve, Susan, Cassie, Barb, Jim, William, Bonnie, Peg, Ron, Diana, Chris, Jill, Eric, Missy, Bryn, Dana, Russell, Laurie, Jay, Sue, Andy, Sofia, and Stella the dog.

From Patrece . . .

Fairy Godmoms turn naturally for messages from Mother Nature, our feminine planet. And to some of my other respected messengers:

Julie: You are my tiger twin who prowls the jungles with me jumping over the traps and using vitality, humor, and curiosity in this never-ending exploration of remindhers.

Tracee: You gave me mom wings that grow larger and larger with each adventure we share. Many others are now in the community of heaven, never more than a breath away in my appreciation.

Those who provide the wind beneath my wings and who cause me to smile whenever they come to mind: Georgette and Bonnie, Ellyn and Ramona, Nanz and Isla.

Barbara, my older sister, who raised four sons as one of many other things she did well all at the same time.

Messengers appear in guise (guys) also: Gregge Tiffen brings the music of the spheres and the colors of the rainbow into focus for our kingdom, a truly benevolent King.

Todd, my nephew and confidante, brings me reminders of the wonder males find upon Mother Earth as sons, brothers, husbands, and fathers.

Sukkid, Andy, and Mohan bring the corners of the Earth together in our home.

Emery, my brother-in-law, brings an appreciation of nature to everyone's attention to enjoy and nurture.

Brian (Julie's husband) leads the way side-by-side with William and my male dog, Wizard and female dog, Tasha.

To those of you who have opened the windows of your soul to me over the past 30 years: You know who you are, you know where you are, and you must know of my ongoing interest and appreciation.

Jake Brenner

Julie and Patrece

Contact Us

What would you ask your Fairy Godmom
if you had five minutes with her?

Email

julie@juliewheaton.com
mpatrece@gmail.com

Snail Mail

Post Office Box 12754
La Jolla, California 92039-2754
Phone: 858-658-0665

Other Reminders

Phenomenal Woman
Maya Angelou

*The Highly Sensitive
Person in Love*
Elaine Aron, Ph.D.

Everyday Sacred
Sue Bender

The Artist's Way
Julia Cameron with
Mark Bryan

*What You Think of Me is
None of My Business*
Terry Cole-Whittaker

*Every Saint Has a Past
Every Sinner Has a Future*
Terry Cole-Whittaker

God's Dictionary
Susan Corso

Circle of Stones
Judith Duerk

I Sit Listening to the Wind
Judith Duerk

The Gift of Story
Clarissa Estes

*Chop Wood, Carry Water
A Guide to Finding Spiritual
Fulfillment in Everyday Life*
Rick Fields, Peggy Taylor, Rex
Weyler, and Rick Ingrasci

Book of Qualities
Ruth Gendler

Excuse Me, Your Life is Waiting
Lynn Grabhorn

*Excuse Me, Your Life is
Waiting Playbook*
Lynn Grabhorn

The Passion of the Possible
Jean Houston

Families
Jane Howard

He
Robert A. Johnson

She
Robert A. Johnson

We
Robert A. Johnson

After the Ecstasy, The Laundry
Jack Kornfield

Holy Bible, from the Ancient Eastern Text
George M. Lamsa Translation from the Aramaic of the Peshitta

Love and Logic Journal
Published by Love and Logic Press, Inc.

Kitchen Table Wisdom
Rachel Naomi

On Becoming a Person
Carl Rogers

The Four Agreements
Don Miguel Ruiz

The Art of Selfishness
David Seabury

O, The Oprah Magazine
Published by Evelyn Seelig's daughter

Passages
Gail Sheehy

New Passages
Gail Sheehy

The Art of Possibility
Rosamund Stone Zander

Stop Improving Your Life and Start Living
Jean Stuart

The Art of Growing Up
Veronique Vienne

www.g-systems.com
Gregge Tiffen